CRITICAL

FOR TRAVELERS

W9-AZK-292

"The *Travelers' Tales* series is quite remarkable."
—Jan Morris, author of *Journeys*, *Locations*, and *Hong Kong*

"For the thoughtful traveler, these books are an invaluable resource.
There's nothing like them on the market."
—Pico Iyer, author of *Video Night in Kathmandu*

"This is the stuff memories can be duplicated from."
—Karen Krebsbach, *Foreign Service Journal*

"I can't think of a better way to get comfortable with a destination than
by delving into *Travelers' Tales*...before reading a guidebook, before seeing a travel agent. The series helps visitors refine their interests and read-
ies them to communicate with the peoples they come in contact
with...."
—Paul Glassman, Society of American Travel Writers

"...*Travelers' Tales* is a valuable addition to any pre-departure reading list."
—Tony Wheeler, publisher, Lonely Planet Publications

"*Travelers' Tales* delivers something most guidebooks only promise: a real
sense of what a country is all about...."
—Steve Silk, *Hartford Courant*

"These anthologies seem destined to be a success...*Travelers' Tales* promises to be a useful and enlightening addition to the travel bookshelves.
By collecting and organizing such a wide range of literature, O'Reilly
and Habegger are providing a real service for those who enjoy reading
first-person accounts of a destination before seeing it for themselves."
—Bill Newlin, publisher, Moon Publications

"The *Travelers' Tales* series should become required reading for anyone
visiting a foreign country who wants to truly step off the tourist track
and experience another culture, another place, first hand."
—Nancy Paradis, *St. Petersburg Times*

"Like having been there, done it, seen it. If there's one thing traditional
guidebooks lack, it's the really juicy travel information, the personal
stories about back alleys and brief encounters. The *Travelers' Tales* series
fills this gap with an approach that's all anecdotes, no directions."
—Jim Gullo, *Diversion*

A MOTHER'S WORLD

JOURNEYS OF THE HEART

TRAVELERS' TALES GUIDES

A MOTHER'S WORLD

JOURNEYS OF THE HEART

Collected and Edited by

MARYBETH BOND AND PAMELA MICHAEL

Series Editors

JAMES O'REILLY AND LARRY HABEGGER

TRAVELERS' TALES, INC.

SAN FRANCISCO, CALIFORNIA

Distributed by

O'REILLY AND ASSOCIATES, INC.

101 MORRIS STREET

SEBASTOPOL, CALIFORNIA 95472

Be like the Mother of the world
who carries the world in her heart.
Awaken with wonder
the child of the spirit
for whom all beings are new.

—SUFI SAYING

*This book is lovingly dedicated
to our mothers and our children—*

Ruth, Annalyse, and Julieclaire

Patricia and Jonathan

Table of Contents

A Mother's World: An Introduction

Men and women share one essential experience in life: each has resided in the womb of a female. No matter what our differences and how wide the gulf of gender, culture, race, class, and time, all of us are woman-born—everyone has a mother. To have lived *inside* the body of another is a profound and unfathomable circumstance.

A mother, on the other hand, remembers all too well what it feels like to have another human being share her body. We are blessed with the long and slowly unfolding knowledge and sensation of carrying life inside us. This remarkable process gives us not only an acute awareness of the connections between all living things, the responsibility inherent in creating life, its fragility and magic, but also the pain and sorrow of existence, the fear and reality of loss.

Yet the physical feat—the miracle—of conceiving and growing a baby and giving birth grants us only an added insight into what it means to be a mother, a few extra points for effort and experience. We can by no means claim an exclusive territory on mothering, for mothering, nurturance, and caretaking are practiced in countless ways by men and women, child and adult, parent and non-parent alike. From a child nuzzling a younger sibling to a college student helping an underprivileged youth, or a bachelor volunteering at a hospice—we are each mother to us all.

And yet, being a mother can render a woman invisible in society, can limit her career choices and advancement, and even diminish her own sense of herself. Nowhere is this more apparent than in the realm of travel literature.

Don't women with children travel? Search the book shelves of libraries or bookstores and you will find volumes and volumes of travel literature. But you will discover very few that depict women traveling with children or experiencing themselves in "mothering" ways, nurturing others, or engaging in other women's mothering experiences. This omission—this whole overlooked, rich realm of travel experience—implies that having children and journeying (beyond traditional vacations) are incompatible.

Most women in travel literature "leave behind" motherhood, children, and family ties when they travel. Women travelers are generally portrayed as childless, solo adventurers—rootless, tough, fearless, competitive, strong, assertive, and brave. Do women really become men when they travel? Is it necessary for a woman to shed all her uniquely female and maternal attributes in order to venture beyond her doorstep?

Women of all ages are traveling in unprecedented numbers to places near and far, alone, in groups, with babies on their hips, or aging mothers on their arms. There are few difficulties, physical or emotional, real or imagined, that they have not encountered, and generally, overcome. Women have learned that being a mother is one of the greatest assets a traveler can have—it makes connecting with other women much easier and, in some situations can provide a patina of respect that can ward off unwanted advances.

Despite all the talk about travel being unsafe for women, we have, in fact, one significant advantage when we travel—we can go to almost any country in the world and look another woman in the eye and not be intimidated or intimidating. We catch a woman's eye across an aisle or a table. Then perhaps a smile or a nod. And soon we are sharing stories or photos of our loved ones.

Almost every woman traveler will tell you that the second question asked of her when traveling is invariably, "How many children do you have?" The first, of course, is, "Where are you from?" Woman to woman, a significant rite of passage is having children—being a mother—and this shared experience opens doors, worlds, and friendships. When a woman becomes a mother she assumes (joyfully or begrudgingly, or both) a bundle of responsibility, duty, and delight that is universally understood by other mothers, one that offers immediate and fruitful ground for sharing. In fact, establishing motherhood "credentials" is often the most meaningful connection a woman will have with others she meets on the road.

A Mother's World dispels the notion that mothers don't weave all their female strengths into the tapestry of their journeys. Not only do the authors represented in our collection travel in a distinctive style, they also record their worldly explorations in a uniquely female voice. (With the wonderful exception of our sole male contributor, who journeys to Alaska to meet his adoptive, and adopted mother's long lost blood relatives.)

These "journeys of the heart" illuminate, celebrate, lampoon, and examine a rich panoply of human experience, often exploring terrain not usually covered in travel writing—a joint decision made in Italy to conceive or not to conceive, camping alone with a one-year-old on the rugged Northern California coast, realizing an aging mother's mortality while trying to navigate a Cairo marketplace, questioning oneself while cradling a dying child at Mother Teresa's orphanage in Calcutta. In Romania and India, loving someone else's child as an adoptive mother, dealing with the pain of leaving a child behind while traveling for business, and the hassles of taking a toddler along to a New York museum. Mother Nature (and mother nature) is revealed again and again in these stories—as goddess, healer, teacher. And finally, mothers speak of the pain of letting go, separation, the empty nest, and the "last goodbye." The combined voices in *A Mother's World* remind us that traveling—like motherhood—is not always easy, but certain to be an endlessly fascinating and challenging experience.

While the human race and the planet itself seem to face new perils, we are also learning how to mother the earth, each other, and ourselves. From struggling to save the snow leopard in the Himalayas, to preserving and restoring the world's rivers, to more conscious and joyous parenting and partnering, we—both men and women—are finding ways to manifest the love, respect, commitment, cunning, and prodigious strength of purpose that mothering and nurturance require. Increasingly, we are beginning to understand that the future rests in the arms of a mother—that, indeed, it is a Mother's World.

—Marybeth Bond and Pamela Michael

* * *

The Willamette

The hardest part of mothering is letting go.

I wanted my daughter to lie in the tent, pressed between her brother and father, breathing the air that flows from the Willamette River at night, dense with the smell of wet willows and river algae. I wanted her to inhale the smoke of a driftwood fire in air too thick to carry any sound but the rushing of the river and the croak of a heron, startled to find itself so far from home. I wanted the chemical smell of the tent to mix with the breath of warm wet wool and flood through her mind, until the river ran in her veins and she could not help come home again. That is why, on the weekend before my daughter left for Greece, I made sure that the family went river-camping on the Willamette.

My daughter comes from a long line of people with strong homing instincts. My daughter's grandmother, my mother, was born in a river town, Thornaby-on-Tees, Yorkshire, in a brick house three blocks from the North Sea. Although she breathed the seaweed wind, she never walked on the beach below the limestone cliff at the end of her street. Warning signs and long coils of barbed wire protected the homeland against German invasion and kept my mother away from the sea.

Her father was one of the few men left at home in England

during World War I. He was a ships' model builder who carved little wooden warships, patterns for the shipyards at Sunderland. Sometimes he brought his work home. My mother's strongest memory of England was the fragrance of fresh cedar curling under his plane and falling in long coils on the kitchen table. As he worked the wood, my grandfather sang Scottish folk songs—*You take the high road and I'll take the low road*—and the Navy hymn, *for those who perish on the sea.*

One night, my grandfather took my mother into the city to see where the zeppelins had firebombed the streetcar barns. Under the cover of darkness, the zeppelins had moved slowly, silently, upriver to the shipyards, following the lights of the ships on the Tees. They dropped their bombs, turned, and ran back to the sea. After that, blackout was imposed, and the zeppelins, when they returned, followed the moonlight reflected on the river. My mother thought how beautiful the river must have appeared to the German airmen, its surface ablaze in reflected light from exploding buildings, and how anxious they must have been to get back home.

After the war, the shipyards shut down and my grandfather—unemployed and uneasy—began to think about emigrating. He argued for America because it was the only country that printed "In God We Trust" on its money. My grandmother refused to leave home unless she could come back to Thornaby-on-Tees every four years for the rest of her life. When my grandfather made her that promise, she gave away everything that wouldn't fit in three tea chests and dressed her children in their best clothes for the trip to America. Their destination was Cleveland, where an uncle had an extra room.

From the day they arrived, the family saved everything they had for four years and then, every four years, spent everything they had saved to go back home. They traveled on the Cunard Line, second class. I have the picture postcards they sent back to America: yellowing photographs of oversized ships lined with tiny people wearing hats and waving. I also have ten teacups, one for every trip. They are decorated with painted ivy or pictures of the Queen. One says, *there'll always be an England.*

When I was first married, we lived in an apartment above a delicatessen in Cleveland. The apartment had a balcony overlooking a major arterial. Evenings, we sat on the balcony in lawn chairs and watched the city life flow out of Cleveland in heavy white cars. One night we drove into the city to see the oil slicks burning on the Cuyahoga River. We couldn't get close enough through the brickyards and factory gates to see the river. But we could see thick black clouds trapped in the rivercourse, glowing red underneath.

We began to think about leaving Cleveland. My husband argued for Oregon, because it had clean, cold rivers. So we moved to the Willamette Valley and made our home here. But I returned to Cleveland every year at Christmastime.

I have a picture in my memory of the drive through darkness to the Portland airport, with white fog flowing down the Willamette River as if even the air ran to the sea. I have a picture of the airport in early morning darkness. People are crowded together with their coats on, some sleeping curled up in chairs, their belongings in piles behind them. Everyone is solicitous, subdued, uneasy, as I

> *I* remember mother telling me to look for the faces of my ancestors in the clouds. Today they are in a rush, scudding by like ponies with long white manes racing for the horizon. In the upper ether the wind is raging, although it barely whispers where I sit. In this stillness I answer to no one except those who preceded me.
>
> The land beneath my feet tugs at me, as roots to a tree. This place resides somewhere deep in my DNA. It must, because I didn't even know my connection to it the first time I came here. It called me, and called again, until finally I answered its pull.
>
> ◆
>
> —Robin Tekwelus Youngblood, "The Place of My Ancestors"

imagine people to have been in the harshly-lit tunnels under London during the War.

Fewer and fewer things drew me back to Cleveland each year, but still I went. At first there was the house I grew up in, and my mother and father and my two sisters, and the carols we always sang after supper. We sang slowly, in four-part harmony—deep, rich, thick Methodist chords. My mother chose the songs and gave us the pitch. "Winds Through the Olive Trees," four verses. And there were the English family foods—roast beef and Yorkshire pudding and decorated cookies between layers of wax paper in the roasting pan. We always took a picnic to the park in the snow, turning the picnic table on its side to shelter us from the wind coming off the lake. And always, there was the same joke about how the house was so full of people that we would have to cut off the back half of the Christmas tree and wedge it up against the wall.

But the house dropped out of the picture when my mother and father moved to a smaller place. My sisters got married and moved to bright new houses in the suburbs near Pittsburgh and Baltimore. Then my mother died. We couldn't pitch the songs. My father got sick. And so the rituals dropped away one by one, until there was nothing left at home except my father and the joke about the half a Christmas tree. Finally, it seemed that the only reason to go home for Christmas was that someone needed to be there to hear my father tell the joke.

I know a biologist who studies the homing instinct in garter snakes. He says that garter snakes spend the winters clustered together in rock piles underground, ancestral wintering dens that may have been home to snakes for a thousand years. In the spring, all the snakes crawl out and travel, maybe half a mile. Each one establishes a home base for the summer, a pile of leaves or the space under a fallen log. They travel out each day, but each night they make their way back home along the same trails. When biologists draw a snake's wanderings on a map of the land, the lines are thick, drawn back and forth, back and forth, like rays extending out from a home base. In the fall, the adults travel back to spend the winter with their relatives in the ancient family home.

Before they return to the den, the females give birth to a pile of lithe little snakes and then move on, leaving the babies to fend for themselves. The babies spend the winter, who knows where. But the next fall, the yearlings travel back unerringly to their ancestral home—a place they have never been. As they go home, they will pass over other dens that would be perfectly good places to spend the winter, not stopping until they get to the den that shelters their own elderly aunts and distant relations.

Scientists know so much about homing in animals: Bees orient to polarized light. Salamanders steer by lines of geomagnetic force. Garter snakes follow scent. Pigeons use the position of the sun. Songbirds follow the stars. They are all drawn to a place proved to be safe by the hard, undeniable fact of their own existence. But who has studied the essential issue: What will draw our own children back home?

By the time we got all our camping gear stowed away in the driftboat, it was late afternoon. In the shadows of the riverside cottonwoods the air was cold and sharp. So we drifted along the eastern bank of the river, glad for the warmth of the low light. We pulled up onto the gravel beach of an island thick with willows and set up the tent on a pocket of sand.

After supper, my daughter and I walked down to the shore. We wore high black rubber boots and walked sometimes in, sometimes out of the water, the round rocks grinding and rolling under our feet. Far ahead, a beaver slapped its tail against the river. We talked quietly—about her visa, about loneliness, about how the skyline of the distant coast range seemed to glow in the dark.

Fog thickened the darkness, so even though it wasn't late, we turned back toward our supper fire. We didn't talk much on the way back, but we sang like we often do along the edge of a river, where the density of the air and the rush of the river make the music rich and satisfying. We sang the "Irish Blessing"—my daughter sang the soprano part—and we did fine, the river singing the bass line, the rocks crunching under our boots, until we

got to the last blessing: May the rain fall softly on your fields. *Then I
couldn't do it any more. I sent my daughter back to the fire alone. I lay face
down on the round rocks and cried until the steam from my lungs steeped
down into the dried mud and algae, and the hot breath of the river rose
steaming and sweet around my face.*

> ——— ☾ ———
>
> *T*he mother-child relation-
> ship is paradoxical and, in
> a sense, tragic. It requires the
> most intense love on the moth-
> er's side, yet this very love must
> help the child grow away from
> the mother, and to become fully
> independent.
>
> ◆
>
> —Erich Fromm

Maybe the homing in-
stinct is driven by traditions:
hanging Christmas stockings
each year on nails pushed
into the same little holes in
the mantel. Maybe it is driven
by smells or tastes or sounds.
But maybe the homing in-
stinct is driven only by fear.
On the road, at dusk and
away from home, the fore-
boding, the oppression of un-
defined space, can be unbear-
able. Pioneers knew this
dread; they called it *Seeing the elephant.* Starting out, the wide open
spaces were glorious—the opportunities, the promise, the prairie,
all fused with light streaming down from towering clouds. Then
suddenly the clouds became an elephant, a mastodon, and the
openness turned ominous. The silence trumpeted and the clouds
stampeded. Dread blackened the edges of the pioneers' vision.
They saw the elephant and turned their wagons around, hurrying
through the dusty ruts back to St. Louis. They had to go back.
They had to get home.

The French existentialists knew that feeling, *la nausée*, existen-
tial dread. The pioneers—they, we—walk out into a world we
think makes sense. We think we understand what things are and
how they are related. We feel at home in the world. Suddenly,
without warning, the meaning breaks off the surface, and the truth
about the world is revealed: nothing is essentially anything. The
prairie gapes open—"flabby, disorganized mass without meaning,"

Sartre said. Pioneers can create meaning by their decisions, but those decisions will be baseless, arbitrary, floating.

This discovery comes with a lurch, thick in your stomach, like the feeling you get when you miss a step on the stairs. When the feeling comes over you, you have to go home, knowing that home doesn't exist—not really, except as you have given meaning to a place by your own decision and memories.

Robins singing woke me up in the morning, a whole flock of robins at the edge of the Willamette. Each robin was turned full into the sun. I climbed out of the tent and sat cross-legged on the gravel, my face turned toward the warmth, my eyes closed, bathed in pink light. Soon my daughter, in long underwear and rubber boots, ducked out of the tent and walked to the river to wash her face. She scooped up a pot of river water and carried it to the kitchen log to boil for tea. Crossing to the campbox, she rummaged around inside until she found matches, scratched a match against a stone, lit the stove, and set the teapot on the burner. Then she sat on the broad log in a wash of sunlight, pulling her knees up to her chest and tilting her face toward the light. Her hair, in the sun, was as yellow as last winter's ash leaves in wind-rows on the beach.

Scientists say that a wasp can leave its hole in the ground, fly from fruit to fruit, zigging and zagging half the day, and then fly straight home. A biologist once moved the three rocks that framed a wasp's hole and arranged them in the exact same pattern, but in a different place. The wasp landed between the rocks, right where its hole should have been, and wandered around, stupefied.

My three rocks are the Willamette River. Whenever I walked out of the airport, coming home from a long visit to my father's house, I could smell the river, sprayed through sprinklers watering the lawn by the parking lot. The willow-touched water would wash away the fumes of stale coffee and jet fuel and flood me with relief. This is what I want for my daughter.

Kathleen Dean Moore is the Chair of the Department of Philosophy at Oregon State University. Her essays and articles have appeared in North

American Review, Northwest Review, Willow Springs, *and* The
New York Times, *among others.* Riverwalking, *from which this
story was excerpted, is her first collection. She lives with her family in
Corvallis, Oregon.*

★

He says that woman speaks with nature. That she hears voices from
under the earth. That wind blows in her ears and trees whisper to her.
That the dead sing through her mouth and the cries of infants are clear
to her. But for him this dialogue is over. He says he is not part of this
world, that he was set on this world as a stranger. He sets himself apart
from woman and nature.

And so it is Goldilocks who goes to the home of the three bears, Little
Red Riding Hood who converses with the wolf, Dorothy who befriends
the lion, Snow White who talk to the birds, Cinderella with the mice as
her allies, the Mermaid who is half fish, Thumbelina courted by a mole.
(And when we hear in the Navaho chant of the mountain that a grown
man sits and smokes with bears and follows directions given to him by
squirrels, we are surprised. We had thought only little girls spoke with animals.) We are the bird's eggs. Bird's eggs, flowers, butterflies, rabbits, cows,
sheep; we are caterpillars; we are leaves of ivy and sprigs of wallflower. We
are women. We rise from the wave. We are gazelle and doe, elephant and
whale, lilies and roses and peach, we are air, we are flame, we are oyster
and pearl, we are girls. We are Woman and nature. And he says he cannot
hear us speak.

But we hear.

—Susan Griffin, *Woman and Nature: The Roaring Inside Her*

CHERILYN PARSONS

* * *

Mother to the World

Not all mothers bear children.

I AM FEEDING A CHILD IN SHISHU BHAVAN, MOTHER TERESA'S orphanage in Calcutta. I give him tiny spoonfuls so he won't choke on this stew of rice, carrots, peas, and curry that the Missionaries of Charity have prepared. I cut the carrots, keep the food towards the end of the spoon, and wait until he swallows before giving him another bite. It is taking over an hour to feed him.

His giant brown eyes, fringed with lashes, move from the food to my face as if he needs my gaze as much as the rice. I'm keeping tears down, intent on doing this work. He has a huge belly from malnourishment, spindly limbs, and a tiny chest racked with advanced tuberculosis. Except for opening and closing his mouth, he is very still. It's impossible to tell his age. He looks about a year old, but I was told by the Sisters that he is probably four or five. He has no name.

It's the middle of heat season. I smell the fetid odor of this child's flesh. His urine flows like water through his body, which doesn't remember how to absorb. I smell my own body, damp and dirty in the sweltering humidity. Sweat drips between the crooks of my elbows and knees as I sit cross-legged in my cotton dress. I feel faint from this heat but keep lifting the spoon, my eyes riveted on this child who depends utterly on women he doesn't know.

This ageless, nameless boy was left abandoned on Mother Teresa's doorstep, as many children are. Perhaps this boy's biological mother is dead, or simply so poor that she couldn't care for him—except by leaving him where he might have a chance of life, or at least a more comfortable death.

My first days volunteering for Mother Teresa were spent playing with the older children before I was trusted in the nursery. The older children are long-term residents at Shishu Bhavan. They range from about three years old to twelve. A vibrant, demanding girl named Radha seemed determined to walk (and fall) in spite of her polio. Leaning over to hold her up, I walked her around the room so many times that my back ached. Then I carried other children whose polio was so bad that their legs hung thin, soft, and useless. I held Dasa at the window for hours, my arms cradling him carefully so I wouldn't crush his limp legs. He loved to play with the latch and figure out how it worked. Some of the children are mentally disabled, and they cry and hit when I set them back down after holding them. Two girls are blind and beat their fists on their heads and ears as if to stop a terrible din inside.

I've changed numerous diapers made of *lunghis*, the triangular scraps of cloth that men all over India wear. No Pampers here, wicking away moisture to keep bottoms dry. The *lunghis* are made of cloth woven at Titagarh, a nearby colony operated by Mother Teresa that houses people healing from leprosy.

Calcutta is the most intense, horrible, wonderful place in the world because it forces you to ask not only what life means, but what your responsibility is to life. When I walked into Shishu Bhavan for the first time, I was overwhelmed by tenderness, outrage, exhaustion, impotence at these problems, and anger at the parents and society that create such anguish. I was dazed at the complexity of issues that build this orphanage as surely as bricks do. I was appalled at the Catholic Church and Mother Teresa for resisting birth control. Stunned at the compassion of the nuns in serving these children. Upset at how limited their response could be: these still aren't happy kids.

Most of all, I was thrown back to stare at what my response should be to the world, especially as embodied in the lives of children. The fact that I am a childless woman doesn't matter; and if I were a man it wouldn't matter either. We all give birth to the world around us.

Sister Charmaine, who runs Shishu Bhavan, said to me, "What matters is for each of us to do what we can. And what is that? Isn't it love? Isn't that all? To do that however we can?"

But what does love mean? Why was I volunteering here? It had taken me a week after arriving in Calcutta, the halfway point on my round-the-world journey, to gather the courage to inquire about working for Mother Teresa. I felt shy about trying to love, if that's what I could call it— about believing that I, a young professional from Los Angeles, would have anything to give the struggling children in Shishu Bhavan. I couldn't presume to be a mother, much less a Missionary of Charity. Surely I was just assuaging guilt. My volunteering probably would help me far more

> ——— ☽ ———
>
> For millennia women have dedicated themselves almost exclusively to the task of nurturing, protecting and caring for the young and the old, striving for the conditions of peace that favor life as a whole...to the best of my knowledge, no war was ever started by women. But it is women and children who have always suffered most in situations of conflict. Now that we are gaining control of the primary historical role imposed on us of sustaining life in the context of home and family, it is time to apply in the arena of the world the wisdom and experience thus gained in activities of peace over so many thousands of years.
>
> ◆
>
> —Aung San Suu Kyi, in a speech at the 1995 Beijing Women's Conference

than them. And my gift was nothing compared to the suffering that India makes you see.

But traveling itself makes you see, too, not only what is outside but what is inside. Travel is about transformation. It is about discoveries of all sorts. It was easier for me to jump alone on a bus to a remote village—an act that many people would call courageous—than to travel the inner territory where my heart might be broken and I just might grow up. I had to try.

I walked through the congested, filthy streets towards "the Motherhouse" to inquire about volunteering. The street numbering wasn't clear, but everyone knew how to find "the Mother." I turned down a mud alley off a busy street. A little brass card saying "M. Teresa" and "Sisters of Charity" marked the door of an undistinguished three-story building with brown wooden shutters.

Sister Dolores, the Volunteer Coordinator, gave me a cordial and businesslike welcome. In the plain rooms, which were furnished only as much as needed, was serene activity. The house was built around a large courtyard where other Sisters were doing laundry in large buckets. Some of the women wore white cotton saris edged with blue, while others had plain white saris. The women themselves were brown, yellow, white, or black skinned.

Sister Dolores heard my concerns. The cloth draped over her head framed clear, dark eyes. "The Mother says that if the volunteers gain more than they give, that is fine," she explained in lilting, formal English. "It is beneficial simply to be a witness to the work, even for a single day. Then you can use it in your own home, can you not?"

She waited for me to answer.

"Yes," I said. It felt like a commitment.

"There is nothing wrong with gaining spiritually because this kind of gaining does not take from other people—but wants to give even more."

I thought of my life at home and the hoarding of things, experiences, money, and favors, as if fearing that someday there might not be enough. I seemed to assume life was a zero-sum game—wasn't it?

"The Mother is out right now but will be here on Saturday," Sister Dolores said.

"You might be able to meet her at Mass then. You are always welcome to join us."

I wasn't Catholic or even religious, but I decided to go to that Mass. And I signed up to work at Shishu Bhavan, the orphanage for disabled, sick, and dying children.

The Missionaries of Charity also invited me to visit Titagarh, the leper colony, which proved to be the cleanest and one of the happiest places I'd seen in India. Most of Titagarh's men and women had lived ordinary lives with good jobs before leprosy struck and they were cast out. At Titagarh they wove cloth for Mother Teresa's missions and formed new families—what we might call "non-traditional families." Though they received medicines to cure their leprosy, the stigma remained, and so did they. Their gardens were filled with vegetables and flowers. The buildings were a rainbow of colors. A school on the grounds served the children of residents, or children with leprosy themselves. Everyone acted as these children's mothers and fathers.

In the evenings in my air-conditioned hotel, I read books on Mother Teresa. "Being unwanted," she said, "is the most terrible disease that human beings can experience.... Today it is the greatest disease, to be unwanted, unloved, just left alone, a throwaway of society.... In the West, there is loneliness which I call the leprosy of the West."

Leprosy eats at the body. The polio of the children in Shishu Bhavan had left them unable to move. I had embarked upon my long trip because anxiety was eating at me. I had felt paralyzed. My boyfriend didn't seem to be the right partner to start a family. I had a job I didn't care about. What was my purpose, my meaning? On my breaks from Shishu Bhavan I wandered the wrenching streets of Calcutta: pandemonium outside, just like I felt pandemonium inside.

Oh the heavy air! I swam through the city, sliding, gasping through the heat; leapt from dry spot to brick on the streets to avoid the puddles and mud; pushed through masses of people

crowding narrow sidewalks lined with sizzling pots and ovens selling *pakoras*, sugar cane juice, rice, and something curried that was
wrapped in giant flat leaves. I had to keep my eyes on the ground
to avoid stepping in feces—
from cows, dogs, humans—
mingled with mud and pools
of greasy frothy water. Little
stinging insects flew through
the air to get into my clothes.

I gave a five-rupee coin to
a woman beggar with a baby
on her arm then fended off
others who ran to me, be-
seeching, flinging their silent
babies in my face. A thin old
man who resembled a dia-
gram of muscles and skeleton
ran like a horse as he pulled a
rickshaw. The Bengalis, the
intelligentsia of India, hung
onto buses inching through
gridlocked   intersections.
Slums seethed outside the
city center.

The city had been called
"Calcutta" thanks to a mis-
pronunciation by the English
of the city's real name: Kali-Kata, named after Kali, the fierce
Hindu goddess who still demands and receives sacrifices of blood,
the symbol across all cultures of the terrible power of the female,
capable of menstruation and childbirth. She is worshipped by
thousands who chant "Kali Ma, Kali Ma"—Mother Kali—and
heap garlands of beautiful flowers over her savage face. They
shower her with rice, a symbol of nourishment. Kali is the inter-
section of love and ferocity, the essence of a mother. She would be
impatient, I knew, with my despair.

I asked our taxi to return
for us at 7:30 a.m. He
agreed and asked for no money,
he'd collect the fare for the
round trip when he dropped us
back at our hotel. Trust is as
common in India as distrust is in
most places.

It was one of the most amazing
truths I was learning about this
astonishing, baffling, intoxicating, chaotic country with its
5,000-year-old culture, 330 million gods and more than 950
million people.

◆

—Alison DaRosa,
"Rainy Trip to Taj Mahal a
Shining Experience,"
The San Diego Union-Tribune

On Saturday, I walked across the city at five o'clock in the morning to attend the Mass. The Sisters filed into a room on the second floor of the Motherhouse. I had learned by now that the blue-edged saris belonged to fully-ordained Sisters, while a plain white one meant that the woman was still a novice, not yet having taken her final vows. I had also heard that Mother Teresa once declined an invitation to meet the Pope when he asked that she wear a regular nun's habit instead of the sari.

I sat with the novices on the floor, my eyes searching for Mother Teresa—Nobel Prize winner, saint of the gutters, organizational genius who had built an empire of missions around the world but owned nothing. Many people, including me, disagreed with her doctrine, but that didn't seem to matter: merely the mention of her name or the sight of one of her white-clad nuns could part the chaos on a street in Calcutta like Moses parting the Red Sea.

I saw a tiny woman bent almost double walking in with some of the Sisters. She sat on the floor among them, not distinguishing herself in any way. As she lifted her head to greet the women around her, I saw that this was Teresa. Her face was carved deeply with wrinkles. It was difficult to see her expressions because the light was low and her head was bowed as the Mass began: a male priest, the only man present, leading the service.

The Sisters were murmuring, chanting, and praying: Lord, give me strength; Lord, let me see you in the poor, in everyone, everywhere. The god to whom these women prayed was male, but I closed my eyes and felt the presence of the female. India is the only country in the world where most of the people still worship goddesses, whether she comes in the form of Lakshmi, the goddess of wealth in all its manifestations; Durga, the protectress who slays demons; Kali, power; Saraswati, wisdom; Parvati, beauty; or the holy river Ganges, goddess incarnate bestowing salvation—salves to our suffering. The force of the universe is called Shakti, the primal female energy as expressed in a woman's potential to give birth—the gift of life, the world itself. All of India is a Motherhouse.

So what does it mean to be a mother? On my last day in

Calcutta, as I'm feeding the dying child, a single grain of rice falls off my spoon to the floor. I don't notice, but the boy does. His hand seizes the grain and thrusts it into his mouth.

That second, my heart breaks open. I ask: am I worthy of the trust of a starving child who notices when a single grain of rice falls? Do we, both women and men, dare open our hearts to all human beings? There is no greater aspiration, no better journey.

Cherilyn Parsons started writing when she was five and traveling alone when she was nineteen. She has a Masters in Professional Writing from USC and has ghostwritten books, written and edited a variety of articles, and taught at universities—all to support the habit of hopping a plane to travel. She also holds a long-running conversation "salon" from her home in Santa Monica, California. Currently she is writing a novel set in Nepal and northern India.

★

The great Hindu temple of Pashupathinath stands on both banks of the sacred Bhagmati River. Indra, my son Jim, and I walked down the congested dirt pathway to the stone bridge across the rushing brown waters of the river. On the left side of the bridge naked little boys and scantily-clad little girls jumped and dove into the river, shrieking with excitement and joy. On the right side a series of burning *ghats* stretched into the distance. The feet of the body just below us—not yet touched by the flames—were sticking out of the burning pile, toes pointed skyward. Jim glanced down, then turned sharply away, distressed by the scene. Why wouldn't he be? In the prime of his life at forty, death in any form was not acceptable to him. I on the other hand—with more than seven decades behind me—found it, in some way that I did not fully understand, not only acceptable but satisfying, even reassuring. Life and death, not isolated from one another in fear, grief or horror, just accepted, each a part of the same process.

—Betty Ann Webster, "Pashupathinath"

JANET STRASSMAN PERLMUTTER

* * *

Where the Desert Blooms

The author searches for a miracle
at Rachel's Tomb.

IT HAD BEEN A MISERABLE YEAR. CALENDAR PAGES WERE CRAM-
med with medical appointments. Insensitive doctors, fruitless pro-
cedures, and disappointing lab results marked each passing month.
All in the quest for motherhood.

The worst assault was the medications—meant to prime my
body for well-timed ovulation, they succeeded only in lowering
my sullen mood into darker shades of blue.

Travel, often a respite I welcome, left me snarly and out of sorts.
At a *t'ai chi* retreat I fought with the instructor, happier to hide in
my airless tent. I grumbled through Toronto and begged to end the
trip early. Even walks in the woods left me argumentative and tear-
ful. And visits with family raised the uncontainable envy I felt for
siblings who sired children with apparent ease. I had to face it—I
was least miserable just staying home.

I suppose I should have viewed with caution the sudden invitation to Israel: What if the unfamiliar surroundings aggravated my
depressed state? How would I tolerate prolific families of younger
cousins, eager to introduce me to their infants and toddlers? But
these questions didn't arise. All I thought of was the nineteen years

since I last visited Israel, homeland of my Jewish roots and home to a family of favorite cousins.

The impetus for the trip was a bar mitzvah. My husband's nephew would celebrate his coming of age in Jerusalem, and my mother-in-law had offered to subsidize our trip. How could we refuse? I called my beloved Aunt Esther, near Tel Aviv. "We're coming to visit!"

In a schedule marked by monthly ordeals with the fertility specialist, I remember our flight arrangements like this: We would fly out after my November procedure, spend two weeks in Israel, a few days layover in Copenhagen, and return in time for my December evaluation. I hoped I could put aside my campaign for fertility during the weeks we would be away.

Shortly before we flew out, my friend Sue called. "Of course you'll go to the Tomb of Rachel," she said. I had no idea what she was talking about. "That's where women go to pray when they're trying to get pregnant. You have to go."

Rachel, biblical matriarch, had suffered with infertility and struggled severely in childbirth. A tradition had developed among Jewish women to pray for children at the grave site of our foremother Rachel.

---

*T*he name Rachel translates as "mother-love," "womb," or "compassion." It is symbolized by the Divine Ewe, mother of the Holy Lamb in early Hebraic matrilineal tribes.

◆

—MB & PM

I looked at a map. The Tomb of Rachel was just a short drive from where we would stay in Jerusalem. Perhaps we could get there. There was just one glitch—Rachel's Tomb is in Bethlehem, across the "green line," in the disputed West Bank. I decided I'd assess the situation when we got to Jerusalem.

Israel is a compelling place. In Israel I feel at home even in neighborhoods I've never before encountered. While walking its streets my use of Hebrew returned to me and songs I had not sung in years filled my head as if tuned to a Hebrew oldies station.

We toured. We visited. We enjoyed the bar mitzvah. We traveled by public buses and got around Tel Aviv and Jerusalem with relative ease. My mood was light for the first time in months.

Midway through our stay, my aunt cleared a full day to take us around. "Is there someplace special you would like to go?" I wasn't sure I could tell her. I had a tough enough time sharing my frustrated efforts to conceive, much less asking this favor in the same breath. My gentle, sixty-some-year-old aunt who traveled only in the safest of neighborhoods—what would she think of a quick trip into Palestinian-dominated Bethlehem?

Hesitantly, I queried. Aunt Esther consulted with Uncle Muni. Just as her kids had predicted, she couldn't say no. She and Uncle Muni and the twenty-year-old Volvo would meet us in Jerusalem mid-morning.

My recollections of the short drive are fuzzy. I'm sure I expected something dramatic. Mostly there was a patched two-lane road, overgrown grass, and some barbed wire leading up to the kind of border patrols that are not uncommon on Israeli roads. We saw nothing glamorous in Bethlehem—an appliance store, kids on bicycles, women carrying groceries through dusty streets. My uncle parked near a low, stone building, remarkable only for the number of Israeli soldiers at its gate.

We covered our heads, as is the tradition upon entering a Jewish place of worship—scarves for the women and hats or skullcaps for the men—and took a few steps down into the simple building representing Rachel's burial place. We picked up prayer books and followed the buzz of personal prayers into the next room. The bare space was divided by a curtain, men on the far side, out of view of the women near the entrance.

The room was memorable for its sounds, the low mumbling of prayers, interrupted by occasional wailing. I searched for a secluded corner. Not finding one, I stood among the other women and opened my book to the familiar morning prayers.

My aunt handed me a paper with a prayer written in Hebrew.

As far as I could translate, it asked that—on the merits of our matriarch Rachel and other deserving women—God fulfill my wish for a child. Or perhaps that was what I read into the words. I thought of the warm generosity of my grandmothers, of my prayerful great-grandmother, and of my quietly spiritual aunt praying nearby. I envisioned my mother, bearer of seven healthy children. I tried to conjure up the goodness of foremothers I knew only from biblical study. I prayed that by the grace of their virtues God would grant my husband and me a child.

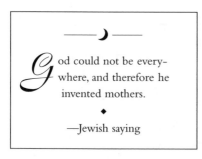

God could not be everywhere, and therefore he invented mothers.

◆

—Jewish saying

I believe in prayer and had been praying for a child for many months. Perhaps something about this sacred place would enhance my pleas. As we left, my aunt told me she had been here once before, with a dear friend praying for her daughter-in-law. By the time her American friend's visit had ended, her daughter-in-law was expecting.

Maybe it was the prayers. Maybe it was the pills. Maybe it was the power of connection with the women of history and the women at Rachel's Tomb, sharing the same desire. Maybe it was the hope I found when my cousin, an Israeli obstetrician, told me that my particular condition was quite responsive to treatment—something my own doctor had failed to say. Two of my Israeli cousins, it turned out, had gone through a similar medical course when first trying to conceive and now had seven children between them.

I will never know which were the critical factors, but my next doctor's visit showed the first signs of progress in nearly two years. One month later I was pregnant.

We named our daughter Eliana. It's a Hebrew name, meaning "God has answered." And she is the most perfect fulfillment of a prayer I could ever imagine.

Janet Strassman Perlmutter juggles travel, writing, and a family therapy practice with the joys and challenges of parenting. She lives in Hopkinton, Massachusetts, with her most dedicated supporters and favorite traveling companions: her husband and daughter. She wrote her first travel article by putting her infant in the car, driving until the baby slept, and writing from the first available parking spot.

✳

Spring dusk. It is the blue of a smoking engine out there, and now, from the pond, the rippling sexual sobs of wood frogs, bullfrogs, the full-throated breathing of the deep night, begin. It is a song so powerful I lay upon the bed pressed into the waves. The air throbs, filled and running over with alluring Spanish *r*'s. This is the night in its entirety—leaves, grass, quaking air. The sound inhabits me, as if the dark passes into me, thrilling and complete. I walk out at midnight to stand within the tension as the moon shows, gleaming and porous, through the stanchions of pine.

Black stalls housing horses, black grass, black trees, whir of black wings at the back of my head. Waking in the deep blackness, nursing a baby, is the most sensuous of animal tasks. All night I wake, feed our baby, sleep, wake again to the tiny body curled to me in the depth of that seething music.

—Louise Erdrich, *The Blue Jay's Dance: A Birth Year*

IRENE-MARIE SPENCER

* * *

The Fourth of July

A mother reflects on her independence.

THE PORCH IS A PLACE OF WORSHIP, WITH ITS FILTERED STREAMS of light eroding all thoughts of my self. The truth of my bare feet becomes clear; they are hinged with flaking cracks and a swollen mosquito bite erupting from my ankle. A child's davenport and rocking chair sits on the white porch, next to my old wicker rocker. Where my daughters sit and sing, grow, cry. Birds hidden in the trees (we've carefully obscured the feeder with branches) are grey and white in the soft down beneath their wings. They make me think of Elsie's soft baby flesh, her little smile.

We have moved to the Midwest, a place about as foreign to me as Hong Kong might be. In fact, I had just finally begun to feel the ability to hold course with any of these Midwestern women. Their nice-from-a-distance and seemingly down to earth manner had fascinated me at first, and had been something unattainable, even mysterious. It was mysterious because it was so different from the California manner I had grown up being accustomed to. The Midwestern personality had at first seemed a flood of human kindness and concern, an unspoken ability to commune with the simple things of life, what I thought of as farm ways. But after having lived for a couple of years in Michigan, and now Wisconsin, I began to feel more like them. Something in me had softened and become more nice. I wasn't sure if this was a good or bad thing. As I examine this more closely, the seeming personableness of these Midwestern women sometimes seems to cover up a feeling I get that something lurks deeper behind the friendly demeanor. Is it a fear, or a mask? A fear of coming out of the niceness. I am never sure what that inner reality was. It is just the feeling that someone can always be friendly and hospitable, even if they don't feel that way. That is kind of scary.

My surfer-beach girlhood is far behind me now; ovenlike after-noons surrounded by pure sand and hot wind, then the bracing cold shock of the Pacific Ocean on my goose-pimply and lithe body, barely covered by the tiniest bikinis I could find. I'd be hard-pressed to get into a one-piece now. And lake swimming just isn't inspiring enough to motivate me to do something about it. Three daughters and fifteen years later, I find myself reflecting pure white, the color the landlord agreed to paint this screened-in front porch in this south-central Wisconsin town I hesitate to call a city. Wisconsin is not a place I would have ever believed I would find myself, yet here I am, and it's the Fourth of July.

The ferns are godlike in filtered sunlight. Raw thyme, craggy in its barren pot, the purple spikes faded, sends me tumbling heart akimbo to Provence, before motherhood, hiking down that vast sea of purple hills loaded with bees...green, hot sun...to come upon a blueness so glorious, so thick and deep I gasped out loud. A man wearing a white cap and driving a convertible with the top down picked me up, whizzing past Romanesque stone churches and small cafe-bars, and drove me to the sea. I hated St. Tropez and didn't stay there. I favored towns like Sisteron; medieval villages in the middle of nowhere overlooking a river, where nothing hap-pens all day. He sat at an umbrella table with a *pain au chocolat* and struggled with a map in the wind, laughing into the reflection of my happy thirtyish face in his black sunglasses.

My porch in Wisconsin glows with stars, tiny pinpoints of these memories, shaded areas patched over the arms of my beloved ferns, the primeval ferns, memory sources. I am so full of

love on this porch. It's the Fourth of July, and we didn't make it
to the parade. So we're here, at the lake, baking quiche, cookies,
soaking black beans. The girls will wave their sparklers at dusk in
the reflection of the lake, their expressions mirrored in the shoot-
ing stars emerging from the tips of their fingers. They will become magicians in the wind off the lake, where we live. Where
the mossy lake grass bends around tree roots like hair dripping
over a woman's bent neck.

I go outside, I sit where it is lush beside the earwigs and mosquitoes, and I hang my head down between my legs. I like living
here, in the Midwest, where fireflies prick the edges of my peripheral vision like magic dust, lights from a subterranean world of
dark soil and the winding underground caverns carved by earth-
worms. They have finally gone to sleep and I feel like walking
through the trees, being bitten by the mosquitoes, to the old dock
where nobody goes. That dock is submerged now, with the rains
and flooding and high level of the lake. The lake is overflowing its
borders now, inundating the seeping edges and tree roots, the small
piers and rowboats are sinking—nobody hangs out there. I live on
the other side of the big lake, where the lushness reminds me of a
tropical coastline so beautiful I cried to be there. That island was
in Sumatra, in the middle of a huge lake, Lake Taupo. A place I visited once, from some distant chapter of my life, a time of enchant-
ment and crystal-clear perception, something much closer to the
childhood I am observing in my own daughters now.

The humidity is deep and fairly uncomfortable, not completely
uncomfortable. It reminds me of the heaviness of the air in
Indonesia. But that was completely different, wasn't it? When you
stepped off the plane in Jakarta, you knew for certain you were
somewhere completely foreign and mystical. The air was different,
it had weight, volume, you could reach out and hold it in your
palm. It enveloped you, you felt dizzy, heady, sexual. This was simply a skinny moist blanket you couldn't kick off, this Wisconsin
humidity. You couldn't shower it off, it just came back before your
hair was dry.

The sweet stench of the northern catalpa blossoms, the white orchid-like flowers infused with sweet sticky nectar, spreads out in a circular fan around the base of the huge tree. Walking beneath the green canopy of branches strewn with white clusters, like orchids, their smell permeating the thick balmy air, I think of losing my virginity. Holding one flower between my fingers, I squeeze out the honey and taste it. The blossoms look like popcorn all over the green grass, a circular white carpet, and my bare toes scatter a few of them as I destroy the perfect circle. The green room, so open and free in my mind, protective like the jungle, papayas bowing the thin branches of their mother trees. Wilderness backpacking…the idea strikes me, the perfect hobby for a woman in her forties who can't stand being a housewife. The more remote and dangerous, the better. White-water canoeing.

I come across an old doll, limbs skewed and partially buried by the delicate white blanket of catalpa petals. These things tell stories, tell of the mysticism of things in life, of childhood, of outgrown shells and needs.

A doll is a mystical thing, a representation of a state of perfection, or the lack of perfection, depending on the kind of dolls one keeps. The dolls that have raggedy, matted hair, dirty faces, broken veins drawn on with purple markers, naked, lying out in the garden, these are the dolls that speak the language of my secret inner life, the chaos, the pain, the unknowing. It's as if those perfect dolls up on the shelves with French lace and pressed dresses and parasols and blond ringlets can only stay on the shelves, or else they get "ruined." Like the dead mouse that once ran alive on our counters at night, eating crumbs freely and drinking leftover juice from half-filled children's cups, he was flattened by poison, stopped dead in his tracks right in between the dishwasher and the refrigerator. I thought perhaps he was alive, but when I touched him with the broom, he was stiff as a dead anything.

Yet all these rocks and shells and pieces of things from the kids, these natural organic things sitting next to things like pink plastic hairclips, a stone full of bubble holes lying next to a silver sparkle

Barbie doll high heel, the discarded pinkish shell of a crab lying next to a cat's eye marble, these things are the stuff of our dreams as they lie next to reality.

I can hardly bring myself to prepare another dinner, after a day wrapped in small legs and arms, white thick vomit the consistency of mucous, small tears that make me remember my mother's aching heart, and my foot punctured by a plastic barn fence. I had crumpled like a huge animal being shot, and howled on the floor as the babies stared at me, blankets in hand.

I must go to her now, my little one, my sparrow…even though she bit my nipple in bed this morning and I had a dream of anger in which I screamed at her, "Little bitch!" For the first time since her birth I felt like slapping her for waking up fifteen minutes after falling asleep for the first time today, at dinnertime. No nap, no peace of mind, not even for five minutes. It's arms and legs and vomit, shit and smiles. God help the mothers of this world. But how could I ever hurt my own sparrows? These tiny women I've been granted the privilege of loving and holding are my closest allies, perhaps my only allies. They are butterflies waiting to be unspun, wet from their baby bodies. Wrapped in blankets, leaves, and filmy gauze, they are the cocoons of lost pieces of my soul. Under the mosquito netting covering the carriage, their eyes flit to and fro in the ravines of light caught in the wicker spaced with blue sky. I teach them to smell herbs, crushing the tiny leaves between their small fingers. I teach them to hold hands, to laugh at the sometimes silliness of men. I teach them about the strength of women, the earth, and rainbow guardians of the world. My own mother let herself be crucified. The point is to step out of martyrdom, proud as a statue towering over Rhodes, and to step along uniquely with the centuries of walking on sand beside the lake. To release the vast and fallow, but hold dear the small and fertile.

If only I could become lost in the minute world I can see in one corner of a cloud, in the edge of a slimy rock by the lake. This miniature world of the dollhouse and the fractal is given easily to the woman, a natural gift. We are born with fractal eyes. Our gaze spins 360 degrees, like the Medusa, encompassing fractals at every turn towards the next periphery. It all begins with the wickered edge of a white bassinet, with the small rooms of a dollhouse, with traces of sand and bone along the shore, the shapes of things. We women are akin to the shapes of things, we are shapes, we live in a world flecked with shapes and landmarks.

This small shape of a woman cradled in my lap against my breast, how does she feel in the rain?

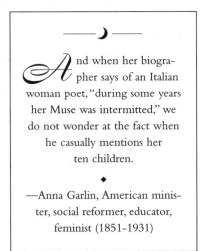

*A*nd when her biographer says of an Italian woman poet, "during some years her Muse was intermitted," we do not wonder at the fact when he casually mentions her ten children.

♦

—Anna Garlin, American minister, social reformer, educator, feminist (1851-1931)

The garden light is fading and the kids are running like colts. They are screaming and their dry legs are white with scratches. The light, too, is dry on the porch. A square patch of gold on the aging botanical print is growing oblong, and I wish I could put it in a box to last forever. A box to open some day and be there again on the porch, inside that eternal moment.

Some of the flowers are dying back, and the water is dark against the sky. The moon is a day shy of full: a golden disc the color of corn rising over the dark silvery lake this midsummer eve. There are so many fireflies…we catch them, Chloe, Ilsa, and I, seeing who gets the biggest ones like lanterns. The pungent scent of the herbs near the shore mingles with the cigar smoke from a neighbor on the other side of Dottie's Boat & Bait Shop. He is sitting out by the lake, enjoying the twilight, as we are, and I water the weedy garden. My garden is untended, like so many other details of my life. I love the descending darkness. This sound of the lake in the dark expands the hearing. It is midsummer, the flowers show it, the fireflies flash this message in the summer night, under the huge firefly of the full corn moon. Something about witches tonight: mysticism. It's Midsummer and

I'm becoming acclimated to the heat of the days, the humidity, the thunderstorms.

Night will fall soon. The sounds of the lake soothe, the voices of birds and ducks in the quickening dusk edging out the paleness of the garden landscape. The garden was the first thing I had looked at in the morning, the moment of coffee and stale bread with cinnamon and sugar, the thoughts of escaping and running out of the house past the garden out to the lake to stare at the silvery water bathing in pinkish morning sun. "The sunrise lake" they call it. Ever since we moved here, I've been waking up at the break of dawn. There is that crack on my paneled bedroom wall, the gold slit of light that projects straight into my mind in the early morning like a sword of light reaping through whatever pale dreams I might be having. But it's Chloe who always wakes first. She was born a dawn riser.

There is a dead lantern hanging there by the big tree next to the lake, a lantern that remembers a golden light to spread across the tender water. This lantern has been forgotten, I'm sure of that. Probably back in the thirties they had lit it on summer nights, had parties here by the lake. I look at my watch. Time to retreat. I sneak around the back of my own house, looking in my windows like a peeping tom. Who lives here? I thought. What kind of life is this? The door to the porch was locked. Foiled, I was forced to enter through the back door, where my husband and the kids stood in the kitchen, heating up dinner. And I thought, belly up, "This is my life. This is the Fourth of July," and acquiesced to the presence of the entire family. We would now light sparklers in the backyard, and I, captain of a great ship of young girls' dreams, would become once again lost to my soul-in-the-woods.

Irene-Marie Spencer, mother of four spirited daughters, attempts to write in her "spare time." She did manage a novel, Tales of the Moon and Water, *while pregnant with her third child and is working on an M.A. in Creative Writing. She lives on a lake in Wisconsin with her family.*

✦

It was May. The sea was turquoise, and the casuarina trees forever sighed. I was tired. For nineteen months I hadn't slept a single night without waking. JJ went to bed when he felt like it. After all, he was nine months old. He'd get up twice to feed, once at eleven and again at four. He waked completely at six a.m. If Daddy wasn't talking to me, I got to bed at ten o'clock. I managed five hours or maybe six of broken snoozes. Once JJ slept all night and I was up seventeen times to see if he was breathing.

I stood there in the hot Bermuda night. It was nearly palpable. I could feel it quivering around me full of centipedes and foolish, breeding people. Groggily, I smoothed my hair. Dad was out. The treefrogs eulogized.

For no reason I could think of I began to cry. I had a sense of desolate aloneness, of being out of whack.

And then, behind me, tentative at first, then rising loud, I heard a howl.

Oh, joy unequaled! The world was stable and secure. JJ was awake again!

—Jean Ann Pollard, "Bermuda Again"

CHRISTINE LOOMIS

✦ ✦ ✦

Vincent's Room

Listening to children can be as subtle or as simple
as seeing an artist's meaning.

WHEN I WAS YOUNG, A TRIP TO THE MUSEUM WAS A SPECIAL, though admittedly somber, affair. My mother and I would walk softly through the vast halls of The Metropolitan Museum of Art in New York City, dressed demurely and speaking in hushed tones of perspective and palettes. We each had an impressive task: I tried to keep my black patent shoes from clicking and echoing too loudly on the great marble squares, and she lectured. My mother loved to stress the difficult years, discipline, and hard work it took to create a masterpiece. I listened. I was even impressed. But the bleakness of her words was always in such contrast to the exquisite and colorful paintings before me. How was such beauty created out of such misery? I decided not to grow up to be an artist after all, since dying, according to my mother, was an all too common prerequisite to appreciation by the masses. Still, I loved to go to the museum.

As with everything else, my mother was very definite about the art she liked and disliked. She dismissed abstract art as not art at all and leaned heavily toward realism. For some reason, however, she forgave the Impressionists their departure from realism in its purest sense—though she continues to shake her head sadly at Monet's last water lilies, which are virtually abstract—and we spent many happy hours browsing among Renoirs, Cezannes, Pissarros, and Manets. To this day, we don't see eye to eye on many matters, including art, but a very special and enduring love of the Impressionists is something my mother and I still share.

Van Gogh was another favorite of mine. As a child I was drawn to his blue, swirling skies and wavy pines that didn't look like any real sky or pine I'd ever seen but seemed incredibly real nonetheless. For that reason I eagerly anticipated the Met's "Van Gogh in Arles" show, and I imagined my husband, Bill, and I walking softly through the great halls, taking in van Gogh's visionary world, and punctuating the educated silence of the exhibit with an occasional sage comment. A lovely scenario, and one my mother would have approved of, but one far from the truth.

I didn't know that, though, when my friend Tina, who worked at the museum, called one day and offered me three tickets for a special pre-opening show of van Gogh. Three tickets—one for me, one for Bill, and, incredibly, one for our daughter, Kira. I admired Tina. I was grateful. I thought her insane. On the other hand, if she was willing to put her job on the line, I was willing to take a three-year-old to a major art exhibit. We had, after all, been taking her to various museums—albeit for short periods of time, at off hours, with no particular destination in mind (the bathroom was the most popular), and with varying success—since she was an infant. So, I thought, why not? I could share with her my love and knowledge—at last, my mother's lectures would really pay off—and she would love what I loved, see what I saw, and come away a better three-year-old for the experience. I altered my scenario to include a nicely dressed Kira trotting obediently around the exhibit, asking perceptive questions about van Gogh to which I would give thoughtful, instructive answers. It would be an enlightening experience for all. It would be the elusive "quality time" parents perpetually seek.

The show was scheduled for 7:30 p.m., not usually the best time for a three-year-old. Undaunted, I filled a bag with juice, a second dinner, extra clothes, a couple of toys, a third dinner (when in

trouble, try food), and a few hundred of the other endless essentials
for kids until we were well prepared for any eventuality, including
flood or earthquake. So what if regular people just reach for a
ticket and trot blithely off to pursue culture in a leisurely, dignified
manner? They're missing something, I thought, still dreaming of a
Norman Rockwell shared family experience. Because it was
windy and cold, I had to scrap the idea of lacy, white ankle socks
and patent leather for sweatpants and sneakers instead. My dream
was well tarnished before we even left the house.

On the way to the museum I tried to prepare Kira. I told her
that an art exhibit was a very grown-up thing to do and that she
had to act very grown-up. She informed me that she didn't have
to because the museum is closed at night. We forged ahead. I half
expected someone at the museum to stop us when we got there,
but whether out of complete ignorance or incredible wisdom, no
one did. After being inside for ten minutes Kira cheerfully acknowledged that the museum was, in fact, open, and we soon
found ourselves at the beginning of the show.

"I want one!" Kira shrieked when she saw the take-along tape
recorders with detailed information about the show piled high on
a table. I tried to explain that the voice on the tape would not be
Cookie Monster or Grover but Philippe de Montebello, the director of the museum, talking about things she wouldn't understand.
Insulted, and therefore obstinate, nothing would dissuade her from
her purpose, and no amount of pleading, ordering, or threatening
would make her move forward without Mr. de Montebello.
Figuring that the first minute of the show was no time for the ultimate power play, we gave in and got two recorders so that I could
listen to one and explain what she was hearing. I was still operat-
ing under the notion that my dream was somewhat intact.

After adjusting the earpieces, which were not designed for
children, off we went into the first room, Kira trotting obediently
beside us, listening intently to her tape. She was apparently fascinated by what she heard. I tuned into mine and was immediately
transfixed by the mellifluous voice of Mr. de Montebello describing the painting before me. The world was shut out and for 30

seconds I counted the exhibit experiment a great success. For 30 seconds. But when it came right down to it, de Montebello couldn't deliver. Oh, he was good, but he didn't have what it takes to hold the attention of a three-year-old for very long. He's no Cookie Monster.

"I'm done," Kira announced.

"What?" I whispered, coming back to reality.

"I'm done."

"With what?" I inquired patiently, fearful of the answer.

"This," she said waving he arm in a semicircle, and dismissing the vision and genius of one man in a three-year-old-sized sweep, she raced into the next room.

Sprinting after her, I tried to explain that one went through an art exhibit slowly, carefully, savoring each painting, but my point fell on selectively deaf ears. I tried a different tack. "Look," I said brightly as we jogged past the flowering orchards of Arles, "flowering orchards." She stared at me blankly and dashed ahead through a crowd of well-dressed art lovers. I tried again.

"There's a beautiful flower," I said.

"I hate flowers," she lied. And the paintings faded behind us. Desperate, I pointed to a river, a boat, a lavender field. But she never stopped moving. We covered the second room in one minute before moving on to the third.

"I'm tired," she whined.

No wonder, I thought, but I was determined to be civilized and patient. Unfortunately, my patience only annoyed her more, and she threw herself on the floor, refusing to move. The embarrassment factor had me strongly in its grip, and if I had thought I could drag a screaming child through a crowd, down a sweeping staircase, and out the door of a museum without anyone noticing, I would have, but no such luck. Every eye turned from van Gogh to me. With no time to pretend that I didn't know the child on the floor, I bent down and tried to force her to stand.

Quick to catch on, she used the old and unfailing trick of making every muscle in her body turn to Jell-O so that nothing on earth could actually make her stand. It soon became clear to everyone that I was not only uncivilized but a failure as a mother. To avoid further embarrassment, I pretended that I was having success with the limp, puddle of child on the floor, and in my calmest, sweetest voice I threatened her with punishment for life if she didn't get off the floor and at least try to appreciate the exhibit.

"Look at that," I said and pointed to a painting. "Look at that. Look at that." But with the same disdain with which she regards peas, she ignored me and van Gogh and climbed up on the leather bench in the middle of the room, stretching out so that no one else could sit down.

My mother never would have put up with it. My mother never would have taken a three-year-old to the museum. Maybe she had a reason, I thought glumly, putting my headphones back on. It was clear that my idyllic scenario had dissolved back in Room One where, according to de Montebello's silky voice, we should still have been.

"I want Daddy," Kira wailed. In complete agreement I marched back to Room Two and dumped her in his arms. They were happy to see each other and I was grateful for the opportunity to slip into the anonymity of adults immersed in culture, breaking the educated silence only for the occasional sage comment.

I heard them coming long before I saw them. "Daddy took me potty," Kira announced loudly to all the assembled cultured masses. There are sage comments and then there are sage comments.

We took turns, picking her up, putting her down, racing through the rooms and back again, sitting on benches, and trying desperately to look at something, anything, in the exhibit. I probably saw the "Van Gogh in Arles" retrospective more times than anyone else in New York, covering most of it as I did four times in less than an hour. Finally, I gave up my lectures. I gave up pointing out "things of interest." I gave up hoping and was utterly defeated. The one good thing was that, at that point, I was too exhausted to care. They say it's always darkest just before the dawn. Well, dawn appeared at last. Out of nowhere, from her reclining position on the bench in the fourth room, Kira pointed to a painting and said, "It's a bed. A yellow bed."

And so it was. We were looking at the famous picture of van Gogh's little bedroom in the yellow house in Arles.

"Whose bed is that?"

Having just moved from a crib to her very own bed, this was a subject that was near and dear to her heart. I told her that the bed belonged to Vincent van Gogh, who had painted all of the paintings.

"Vincent van Goat," she said. "That's a silly name."

"Look," I said, wearily pointing to one of the self-portraits included in the exhibit, the one with the beautiful malachite-green background. "There is Vincent." (We were on a first-name basis, now.) I wasn't all that enthusiastic, expecting, as I was, to be rushed off to parts unknown at any moment. But I had it all wrong as usual. Kira was thrilled. And she was at last still. Suddenly, everything changed for her and for me. The paintings were not just so many rectangles hanging on a wall; they were connected to a man—a man she could see, but more importantly, a man with an interesting bed.

I don't know why I hadn't seen the problem before. After all, I had been a child once. But I had been trying to make my daughter like the things I liked about the paintings, respond to the things I responded to. I saw them, I think—as my mother had—as works of art, created out of years of discipline and misery, and I appreciated them in part because of that. Kira couldn't relate to that any more than I had been able to as a child. To her, they were just pictures of things that weren't that interesting until something clicked. For her, the bed, that image—one she not only understood but which had great personal meaning for her—was the key that let her into the rest of Vincent's world.

"Look," she said to me. "He has his pictures on the wall in his room." I did look, and sure enough, there on Vincent's wall was a picture of the portrait of Eugene Boch—a portrait we had passed in the exhibit earlier. I couldn't believe she had noticed. I know I wouldn't have. "Mom, he has his pictures on the walls," she repeated happily, "just like I do."

He also had a bright red quilt, a nice pillow, a small table and chairs, and a window. Kira liked Vincent's room very much. And she liked Vincent, too. We sat quietly together for a while, then we got up and walked, hand-in-hand, around the exhibit. We saw Vincent's chair, his friends the Roulins ("Madame Roulin with Baby" was particularly interesting), and an old pair of shoes that Vincent hadn't put away. We stood in front of his self-portrait for some time while Kira did some serious thinking.

> *A*rt enlarges experience by admitting us to the inner life of others.
>
> ◆
>
> —Walter Lippman, "The Golden Rule and After," *A Preface to Politics* (1914)

"Mom," she said finally, "did Vincent paint all these pictures?"

"Every one of them," I assured her.

"But who painted him?" And I thought self-portraits were so clear cut. "I can paint myself, too," she said after I explained how self-portraits are made. She was happy that she and her new friend Vincent had so much in common. Finally, we walked into the last room and there was the "Self-Portrait with Bandaged Ear and Pipe."

"Vincent has a boo-boo," Kira shrieked, and all eyes turned to glare at me. This time, I had nothing to be embarrassed about. "How did he hurt himself? Was he jumping on the bed?" she asked remembering, I suppose, how she hurt her head while jumping on the bed.

I decided it was best in this case to cheat a little on the truth and skip most of the stuff about Vincent's mental and women problems and get right to the business about the boo-boo. "He cut his ear," I told her, not mentioning the word *off*. "And then he was very sad," I added, reversing the order of things a bit and omitting the sordid details of the whereabouts of the missing ear. She felt sorry for him because he was so sad, and I was proud of her for her compassion. We went back to the bedroom painting, and I couldn't help but wonder if Vincent had ever jumped on his bed. The culture seekers marched around us silently, making, no doubt, the occasional comment about technique, perspective, and palettes. But their understanding of Vincent, or their reaction to his work, was no better or more appropriate than Kira's, as we sat happily and peacefully in front of the little bedroom.

"I wanted to express an absolute restfulness, you see," Vincent wrote to friend and fellow painter Paul Gauguin about that painting. We did see, Kira and I. Absolutely. When Bill caught up with us, Kira made him see, too. She told him all about Vincent's booboo and his bed. She led him to the pictures of his chair and shoes. She told him all about Vincent, what he did and where he lived. She had a wonderful time. And when we left the show and moved into the room where the books, cards, and posters from the exhibit were on sale, Kira spotted a poster of the bedroom, so we bought it for her. With the poster rolled and tucked neatly under her arm, we strolled home hand-in-hand in the darkness.

Christine Loomis, travel editor of Family Life *magazine and author of* Fodor's Family Adventures, *lives in Boulder, Colorado with her three children. Kira, like her mother's mother, is a talented artist and she rarely puts away her shoes.*

✳

Travel not only takes us into the unknown, it also gives us the distance to see the familiar in a new light. When I took my then-seven-year-old daughter to Paris, I envisioned the city and how we would discover it together. But I learned as much about my daughter and our relationship as I did about the "City of Light."

Tina had declared "No art museums." Since she likes to draw, I didn't take the statement too seriously but figured she just wanted to exert her authority by playing dictator. I insisted, nonetheless, that we stop briefly at L'Orangerie to see Monet's waterlily paintings. While I was awed by the murals, Tina took a quick look around, said "Nice," and was ready to move on.

We saved the best for last. On Sunday, we headed into the French countryside, to Monet's home in Giverny. Without a car, this turned out to be an all-day expedition. Tina had no interest in seeing the painter's house but his garden inspired her. She spent most of our two hours there sketching the tulips, willow trees, and the famous Japanese bridge over the pond. Although she has always loved to draw, her absorption in the land-scape surprised me.

Seeing my daughter in quite literally a different light deepened my perception of her, not only in that moment in Monet's garden but throughout the trip. Thrown into relief against the backdrop of Paris, I saw more clearly her fearlessness, her precocious sense of humor, her fresh per-spectives on art, her feminist sensibility, her stubbornness, her creativity.

—Judith Pierce Rosenberg, "Paris in a New Light"

* * *

Mama Bear

*An adopted son explores the hidden landscape
of his family.*

THE FAMILY IN WHICH I GREW UP WAS MADE UP OF EIGHT COM-
pletely different ethnic backgrounds, four breeding pairs, and fifteen or twenty mixed ethnic origins. Three of the five kids—
including me—were adopted. We seemed to have an endless
number of stories to share, combine, and recreate. My mother told
and retold the stories of our adoptions in exactly the same spirit in
which she recounted the coming of her biological children—with
an eye for the beauty and uniqueness of each child. Her stories
were meant, I think, to teach her children how beautifully different we all were, and how we could laugh at our origins. The
beauty of her children—this was everything to her.

The seven of us laughed at each other's stories while we sat
around the table my parents had ordered, which was specially built
for a family of seven and one guest. I remember wondering if that
one extra place at the table were just in case my mother happened
to find another child looking for a home.

Her inclination toward adoption came naturally. Her upbringing prepared her, in no uncertain terms, for a life of bringing people in. She was half Yup'ik, born in 1929 in a little fishing village
named Kotlik, which is split by a small slough arm of the Yukon

River as it drains into Norton Sound on the Bering Sea. Her mother, Dora, was Yup'ik, and her father was a Finnish trader named Charlie Backlund, who owned the trading post in the village. How the two met is a mystery to me, but he was 40 years her senior and took care of her entire family in hard times. I can only guess that it was a relationship based on necessity.

In the harsh Alaskan bush where the Yup'ik lived, adoption occurred naturally and necessarily. People often died young, leaving their children to be raised by family, friends, or, in many cases, strangers in distant villages. When my grandmother, Dora, died of tuberculosis at the age of 25, my mother moved in with her maternal aunt, Justina. But my mother's journal speaks of the entire village as a family unit that took her in and made her a child of everyone: she was never given the chance to feel motherless.

Her father, Charlie, soon brought my mother and her brother Carl to "the Lower 48," where he hoped they would have a chance for a good education. With his death, which came not long after, my mother was cut off from Alaska and her Yup'ik family for the rest of her life.

She and Carl were adopted once again—this time by Swedish friends of her father's who lived on Vashon Island, near Seattle. The Agrens lived in a conservative, mostly white community that noticed my mother's high, dark cheekbones, her dark hair and eyes. But whether it was because of their connection to

---

A young boy with freckled white skin and light hair ran by.

"You see my boy, Billy. He's my grandson; I adopted him when my daughter died. Two of my own children I gave away when there was little food."

Many of the families cared for children not their own. It was difficult to distinguish who belonged to whom; everybody was related to everyone else in the village.

◆

—Claire Fejes,
People of the Noatak

her father or simply an openness of heart and mind, the Agrens raised my mother to believe she was an Agren.

In the short term this allowed my mother to find home in a foreign place; in the long term it separated her from her beginnings. She became intensely aware of her dark skin, and she tried to hide everything that was native about her. Her mother's picture vanished; her beaded-skin slippers, chewed soft by her grandmother's worn yellow teeth, lay hidden in the back of the closet; her favorite rag doll with black eyes and hair from an Alaskan brown bear "disappeared." She soon blended into the community, and the memory of her old life faded away. She did well in school, grew into a beautiful all-American girl, went to college, became a nurse, and married at 27. Her name, Inaqaq, disappeared with her past, and she became Doris.

I remember Pop Agren, my grandfather, a quiet old Swede with a love for sweets whose eyes sparkled when he looked at my mother. I have no doubt that he loved her as one of his own. Nanna Agren, my grandmother, treated my mother as if she were still the shy, scared Yup'ik child just arriving on Vashon, gently telling her to sit as she pushed plates of homemade raspberry pie in front of her. Nanna died when I was seven or eight and I grieved terribly. Genetic bond or no, I knew I had lost my grandmother. It was my first experience with mourning, an experience that knows nothing of DNA.

The Agrens were a big family—seven, including my mother. I think that's why my mother always wanted to have many children. After marrying my father she gave birth to my two oldest sisters, Michelle and Heidi, but a couple of years later she was diagnosed with a tumor and had a hysterectomy. Her dream of five kids seemed over until she came to the natural conclusion, given her upbringing: adoption.

Four years later she adopted my sister Heather, light-skinned and blond. I wonder if my mother found it strange to think of Heather as her own. I know that the difference didn't matter to Heidi or Michelle. Without morning sickness, swelling, or painful contractions, the family had become one bigger. My mother used to laugh when people asked her if she had missed giving birth to us.

"You must be crazy," she'd joke. "It's the best way to go! You can wake up and say, 'I think I'll have a baby today!'"

And as my father tells it, that's pretty much how I came into the family.

"I was in Washington D.C., on business," he recalls, "and I called home to check in with your mother. She says to me, 'John, how would you like to have a son?' I didn't quite know how to respond to that, but that's OK because she beats me to it with, 'You're now the father of an eleven-pound baby boy!' Just about knocked me off my feet. All I could think of to say was, 'I'll be home as soon as I can.' I wanted to get home before she rushed out and got another one!"

Brad rounded out my mom's magic number, five. I shudder to think what it must have been like for my parents to raise three babies, each within a year of the next, plus two young girls. (Not to mention the three cats, our dog, Flossy, and Heidi's pony, Princess, as well as the entourage of friends who wanted to ride her.) I look at an old black and white photograph of us three youngest with my parents: Heather is giving her camera smile; Brad's lips are puckered with concern and constipation; and I am looking up at my dad, who is looking at my mom, whose smile threatens to swallow us all. This is how I want to remember her, glowing with children, her own, someone else's, any that would come.

Her maternal energy infused our house with warmth, and people and animals of all sorts came and went through our door. One of these people was a man named Al. He was a small, wiry Irishman who loved to speed skate. Every day he'd skate at the rink, doing lap after lap of long, graceful strides, his hands tucked behind him, his body low and angled forward like an arrow. The rumor among the kids was that he had been an Olympic speed skater. He must have been at least 60 then; his hair was silver and his face deeply carved with wrinkles.

I didn't trust Al. He smelled bad, and little yellow flakes fell from his head. He drank too much and told dirty jokes when my parents weren't around. One Christmas I asked my mom why we couldn't have just the family home for the holiday. She looked at me, surprised, and said, "But Colin, all of these people are family, in one way or another."

When my family sat around our dinner table, the topic that came up most often was our genetic history. We took great pleasure in discussing the countries of our origins, and we learned at a very young age that being adopted was a privilege, not a stigma. I knew, for example, that I was half Yugoslavian, and the joke in my family was that everyone in Yugoslavia had huge hands and huge feet. "Land of the bigfoots," my dad always said. I was grateful to also have a quarter each of English and Irish, because I thought that it somehow connected me to my dad's Scottish blood. Brad is half Bohemian, a quarter each English and Irish; and Heather is French, English, Italian, Dutch, Apache Indian, and who-knows-what-else. We three would argue about which of our homelands was the best, and I dreamed of someday going back to the land of the bigfoots.

Mostly I'm content just thinking about the likelihood that somewhere out there I probably do have brothers and sisters who share some of my physical characteristics. As I get older I have more and more questions, and far fewer answers. I love my adoptive family, but the apathy I felt toward my birth parents as a youngster is vanishing, and I want to know who they are. The same thing happened to my mother a few years before she died; Yup'ik voices started calling to her in her dreams, and she would wake up tired and lonely.

My mother died too young, of cancer, when she was 57. She was just beginning to know herself; at least that's what she said in her last days. She wanted to go back to Kotlik and know her Yup'ik relatives; it took her more than 50 years to figure that out. Just before she died she gave me a fetish that a Yup'ik relative had sent her, urging her to return. It is a small bear carved from stone, and strapped to its back with deer sinew is a smaller turquoise arrow. The fetish is supposed to protect the traveler on her journey, and the arrow brings good hunting. I'm not sure why she gave it to me instead of one of her other children. Perhaps she thought that I, her most difficult child, needed more protection in my travels—I was always getting into trouble. Or maybe it was simply intuition. Maybe she knew I'd go to Kotlik.

Two years after her death I clasped the bear in my sweaty hand as I boarded the plane for Anchorage. From Anchorage I caught a smaller plane heading west to Bethel, the city nearest Kotlik. Flying in Alaska was a humbling experience. I expected mountains; instead, I saw rolling hills and flatness, dissected by thousands of frozen rivers and streams, dotted by a million little lakes. It was the largest, emptiest expanse of snow I have seen in my life. Every so often we passed over what looked like a settlement, small clusters of buildings tucked into bunches of trees. Once I thought I saw a person on a snowmobile, a small speck of black moving fast down a river, then swallowed up by the curving whiteness.

The plane began its descent, and up ahead I saw the lights of Bethel. I had never been to a place so far from anything. That night, as I listened to the dogs barking and the sound of sheet metal flapping in the Arctic wind, all my doubts about coming to Alaska began to resurface. What would the people of Kotlik think of me? Would they know that I had been adopted? Would they expect a Yup'ik to walk off the plane? The next morning, I flew due north to the village, the only passenger in a small, single-engine Cessna. Flying over Kotlik, I sensed a seed of loneliness taking root in me; it grew during my stay and has never fully left me. I felt, for the first time in my life, my own smallness; I was a tiny shoot in the midst of immeasurable wilderness.

From the air Kotlik didn't look like much. It ran about a mile down both sides of a tiny arm of the Yukon River. The airstrip sat on one side of the river, the cemetery on the other. There were no cars or streets. A wooden-planked boardwalk connected house to house, school to store, store to house. I saw people gathered at the end of the runway.

As we taxied down the small dirt airstrip, I realized the people were waiting for the plane. Waiting for supplies, I assumed. There were about fifteen of them, all wrapped up in big coats with fur-lined hoods, faces barely visible. Some were hunched and old; a few were children, feet covered in miniature fur *mukluks.*

The plane stopped, and before I was completely out the door I was surrounded by strangers. One man came forward and introduced himself as Matt Andrews, my second cousin. He shook my hand, then shyly and a little awkwardly embraced me. Through his fur hood I saw dark eyes behind thick glasses, black hair, a mustache. His skin was brown and wind-burned. Then he introduced me to the others, who each embraced me in turn. Some said "*wak,*" which means hello, some said "welcome," and one, my great-aunt Justina, said "welcome home." (I learned later that she speaks very little English. She had asked her daughter, Natalia, to teach her those words so that she could greet me properly.) My pack and I were loaded on the back of a snowmobile and minutes later I sat in a warm house that smelled like smoked fish, eager faces all around.

The family is large and complex, and over the next month I struggled to get all the names right, tried to build a family tree. It seemed everyone in Kotlik was related and therefore wanted to meet me: son of their long-lost relative Inaqaq, who left as a child and never came back. They did not seem to notice my whiteness, even though I suspect I was the tallest person Kotlik had seen in a long time. I was a relative, and that was all that mattered.

I was overwhelmed by how firmly my mother had remained in their memory. Justina—her perpetually smiling face crevassed like summer glaciers, her teeth yellow and black like corn—spoke to me in Yup'ik, a clicking and clacking that comes from deep in the throat. Natalia translated. "She says your mother was always quiet and sad, like her father. That he was generous and gave away so much that he was never rich. She says your mother looked like her father. She says your mother was old for such a little girl. She is glad you have come. She says she has been waiting a long time." Natalia finished just a moment after Justina. The room was quiet and I heard the fire popping.

"She wanted to come back," I said, "but she got sick, and…" I didn't know what to tell her, but she nodded as if she understood and spoke again for a moment. Natalia translated, "She says thank you for coming. You are part of our family. It is good that you are home. I am your new grandmother. You must call me grandmother."

I remembered the bear and quickly dug it out of my pocket. Over the last two years it had always been near me. I held it out and showed it to Justina. There was recognition in her face, her lips softened into a sad smile, and small tears formed in the deep creases of her eyes. She took the bear, closed her hand around it, and shut her eyes.

I breathed in deeply, the fish smell new and soothing. In the silence that followed, I let go of my fears and watched my grandmother sleep.

In Native American mythology there are stories of children lost in the wilds and saved by animals. In one of these stories, a young girl is lost while she's playing hide-and-go-seek with her brothers. She is near death when a great bear finds her and takes her home to raise her as his own. Then one day he marries her, and they have children, half-human, half-bear. Years later the brothers kill the bear and take their sister and her cubs back to the village, where she is welcomed by all. But eventually she begins to transform into a bear and, fearing she will harm her family, she takes her children and returns to the wild. I like to think that this story implies a certain power of adoption, of nurture over nature, a belief that our stories define us even more than our genes do. Adopted by the bear, Bear Woman becomes a bear; there is no going back.

The night before I left Kotlik, Justina told me the story of Bear Woman. As she spoke, her old body became young again. Her hands and arms moved gracefully in circles, and her chair wobbled with the motions of her body. Her voice changed pitch dramatically. The clicks and clacks of her voice receded to gentle murmurs as she described the fate of Bear Woman.

The story went something like this: The early morning sky is dark about the sleeping village, though the northern horizon is alive with dancing light. A woman pokes her head out the hide door of her home, looks around, and smells the air. She is afraid, this woman, but somehow strong and determined. Her eyes are sad but fierce. She moves out into the morning, followed by two children bundled up in furs. The three of them move toward the edge of the village, toward the trees and the hill where they picked blueberries that summer. The dogs watch silently as the woman and her children pass, but their teeth show behind curled lips and their fur is erect on the backs of their necks. The woman moves into the trees. Her children wade in her growing footprints as they climb the hill and drop into their home on the other side.

Colin Chisholm is a writer who lives in Montana.

✷

I never saw my mother, to know her as such, more than four or five times in my life; and each of these times was very short in duration, and at night. She was hired by a Mr. Stewart who lived about twelve miles from my home. She made her journeys to see me in the night, traveling the whole distance on foot, after the performance of her day's work. She was a field hand, and a whipping is the penalty of not being in the field at sunrise.... I do not recollect of ever seeing my mother in the light of day.

—Frederick Douglass, *An American Slave*

LOUISE ERDRICH

⋆ ⋆ ⋆

Nests

*Cherished moments are woven
into nature.*

I HAVE ONE NEST OF EASTERN PHOEBE CONSTRUCTION—MUD AND emerald moss, a failed attempt that fell off a too-slick wall, a comfortable looking silver nest constructed of the down of milkweed pods, a loose swirl of long hairs plucked from the tails of our neighbor's brown and white horses. I have the nest of a Baltimore oriole, a long gray sack with a bottleneck, woven to a budded apple branch, a very special nest that my father at sixty-eight risked his neck climbing a high tree to collect for me. I have a tight little nest including plastic tinsel and my mother's pink-blue knitting yarn, a heavy robin's nest of thick muck and flower stems, and a cup of grass and shredded Kleenex. I suppose I could include my wasp nests, the silt cones, the paper bowls, the great gray combed rose I cut from a year-old sumac. I collect nests in late fall when the leaves are off the trees. On my shelves, there are quite a few nests, collected casually year by year. I prize above them all the nest constructed of my daughters' hair.

My mother gave me the idea two springs ago. I saw her draping yarn on the flowering crab apple tree just outside the kitchen window, and the following fall I found the nest containing those very leftovers from a scarf she had been knitting. All last winter, just before breakfast each morning, I brushed the dark brown, the golden, the medium brown hair of our daughters smooth, and all winter I saved the cleanings from the brush in a small paper bag that I emptied by the stump in the yard last spring.

It was not until the leaves fell off and the small trees bent nakedly beside the road that I saw it, a small cup in a low shrub, held in the fork of a twisting branch.

Now, as I am setting the nest on a shelf in the light of an eastern window, our middle daughter's blond hair gleams, then the roan highlights in the rich brown of the eldest's and perhaps a bit of our baby's fine grass-pale floss. It is a tight woven nest that kept its shape through the autumn rain. It is a deep cup, an indigo bunting's watertight nest, perhaps, or a finch's.

It is almost too painful to hold the nest, too rich, as life often is with children. I see the bird, quick breathing, small, thrilling like a heart. I hear it's song, high and clear, beating in its throat. I see that bird alone in the nest woven from the hair of my daughters, and I cannot hold the nest because longing seizes me. Not only do I feel how quickly they are growing from the curved shape of my arms when I am holding them, but I want to sit in the presence of my own mother so badly I feel my heart will crack.

Life seems to flood by, taking our loves quickly in its flow. In the growth of children, in the aging of beloved parents, time's chart is magnified, shown in its particularity, focused, so that with each celebration of maturity there is also a pang of loss. This is our human problem, one common to parents, sons and daughters, too—how to let go while holding tight, how to simultaneously cherish the closeness and intricacy of the bond while at the same time letting out the raveling string, the red yarn that ties our hearts.

Louise Erdrich is the author of Love Medicine, The Beet Queen, Tracks, The Bingo Palace, *and* The Blue Jay's Dance: A Birth Year, *from which this story was excerpted, as well as two volumes of poetry. She is also co-author, with her late husband, Michael Dorris, of* The Crown of Columbus.

★

Now in his twenties, my son Jonathan was an uncommonly direct and sweet young man, kind to women, children and animals, ambitious, but not driven, with a charming and diverse circle of friends, and a characteristic northern California easy-going approach to life. We were just getting used to a new kind of adult relationship with each other when diabetes entered the picture and created new dependencies and fears for us both, tangled us up in heart strings and apron strings, a scared Mama and her boy once again.

I had hoped our trip to Mexico would help us untangle this emotional mess, the challenge of travel being an almost surefire catalyst for confrontation, change, and revelation. We are never more nakedly ourselves than when removed from routine and familiar comforts. The road *itself* is an unflinching ally on a journey of any sort, it had always seemed to me.

—Pamela Michael, "Apron Strings," *Travelers' Tales Food: A Taste of the Road*

* * *

Remembering Dorothy Parker

A daughter searches for meaning
in her mother's past.

MY MOTHER DIDN'T GET HER DRIVER'S LICENSE UNTIL SHE WAS IN her thirties. In Southern California, an endless suburb defined by the automobile, she was never comfortable driving. The only place she drove herself regularly was to the beauty parlor. Like clock-work, once a week, off she'd go in her white 1957 Thunderbird to Mr. Latour's on South Beverly Drive. She drove slowly, intently, clutching the wheel and peering over it, as if afraid that if her at-tention flagged for an instant, the car would get uppity and take off without her. She kept one foot planted on the brake, while the other foot pumped like mad on the gas. I think there was a French poodle on the sign out in front of the beauty parlor, or maybe it was just that Mr. Latour, a small fellow with curly white hair, re-minded me of one.

Her car was a two-seater with what must have been the world's first bucket seats and a removable portholed hood. Needless to say, her style of mothering did not include carpooling. In fact, my mother prided herself on having nothing in common with any of my friends' mothers or with women in general, for that matter. She worked, chain-smoked, and drank her whiskey straight, on the

rocks. While other mothers did their nails, mine was at the studio
with my father writing movies.

I never thought much about how different she was. I just it took
for granted that we had live-in help to do the things that other
mothers did, like laundry, dishes, and bedtime stories. And I was
oblivious to how wooden and tongue-tied my friends became in
her imposing, suited presence.

I only traveled with her once. And although I'm sure my sisters
and my father were there, in my memory it's just her and me.

It's November and I'm eleven years old. We arrive at the L.A.
airport in eighty-degree heat. My white cotton socks keep slip-
ping down inside my penny loafers and the hem of my wool
pleated skirt irritates the backs of my legs. I'm dragging a camel
hair coat, bought specially for the trip. My mother carries a coat,
too. A mid-calf length swirl of black cashmere. She wears a boxy
brown tweed suit with a yellow silk blouse and brown pumps. I sit
beside her as we wait for our flight to be called. Her legs hiss
against each other each time she crosses and uncrosses them. She
snaps open the brown leather purse she holds in her lap and pulls
out a gold compact.

Peering into the little reflection, she quickly runs the powder
puff over her nose. Then she brushes her fingers through her hair
on one side, pushing the short dark curls up and away from her
face. Next, she takes out a lipstick. She opens the case, twirls out
the coral tube, paints her lips and presses them together. I watch,
fascinated that she can do this entirely by feel. She seems completely unaware of me, but when I reach down to scratch an itch,
she raises her eyebrows in my direction, purses her lips, and stiffens
in disapproval.

On the plane, we sit in seats facing each other. I grip the arms
of my seat as the plane accelerates down the runway, faster and
faster, until it lets go and gently rises, little by little, through the
amber, smog-laden air. I turn to my mother to say something. She's
leaning back, eyes closed, her mouth set in a grim line. I remember. She hates to fly. Whenever the conversation turned to air
travel, she'd tell the story of how once, on a transcontinental flight,

she returned from the bathroom to discover that her window had blown in. She said she was bad luck when it came to flying. It sounded like good luck to me. Bad luck would have been if she hadn't had to go to the bathroom just when she did. Gingerly, I touch the edge of the little round window and peer out. As the plane banks and straightens again, my stomach flip-flops with excitement. Below me, the cars and houses grow smaller and dimmer while the sky above grows bluer and brighter.

During the flight, my mother picks at her meal, drinks two Scotch on the rocks, and tucks two more single-serving bottles into her purse. She doesn't relax until the plane touches down in New York City.

We take a taxi to the Algonquin Hotel in the heart of the theater district. In its dark paneled lobby, I fidget in a prickly red chair. My mother drifts through the lobby, stopping to finger the back of a sofa, lingering in front of the framed photographs and clippings on the wall. She stops at a doorway near the back and motions me to join her. We peek into the deserted dining room.

"There—" she says in a hushed voice, gesturing towards a large round table covered by a dark green cloth with a plaque in the center of it, "that's the round table where your father and I ate." The memory makes her smile. "I sat beside Dorothy Parker."

I have only a vague idea who Dorothy Parker is but I know she's a writer, like my mother. I've never met another lady writer. I examine the empty chair, as if it might reveal some secret truth about a woman whom my mother doesn't dismiss with a snort and a witty aside.

"Does she have children?" I ask before I realize the question has even formed itself.

My mother barks out a laugh. "God forbid!"

The next day, we go out to see the City. As I tag alongside feeling unbearably unsophisticated, uncomfortable in my East Coast coat, my mother strides up Fifth Avenue. Her clothes that seem so stiff and off-putting in Los Angeles are exactly right in New York. Disencumbered of a car, she moves with agility through the crowd, impervious to the cacophony of car horns and clouds of bus exhaust. I cling to her as she crosses streets against the lights, terrified that we'll be arrested for jaywalking. We wander through Saks Fifth Avenue, FAO Schwartz, and Tiffany's. At Delman's, the only place in the world, she says, where she can find shoes that fit her narrow foot, I perch on a white brocade chair while she tries on pumps. We walk around the lobby of the Plaza Hotel so I can see the home of Eloise. In my memory, it's all red and gold, hushed, and padded. We walk past arched doorways framed by potted palms. I inhale the perfumed wake of fur coated ladies and watch uniformed porters soundlessly push piles of luggage across the plush carpet.

Then we head across 59th Street to Rumplemeyers, an old-fashioned ice cream parlor opposite Central Park. All marble, wrought iron, and brass, it breathes cool, malt-scented air into our faces as we push our way through the revolving glass door. As I eat a hot fudge sundae, my mother sips coffee, very light and very sweet, the way she likes it. She lights a cigarette and takes a deep drag, tilts her head back, and shoots a stream of smoke towards the ceiling.

"You like New York a lot, don't you?" I ask.

She's quiet for a moment. "I do," she says, taking a quick drag and exhaling. "It's home."

I hunker down over my ice cream as the words sting. If home is here, then what's the place I call home?

"And what's your opinion, madam?" she asks with mock formality.

Dorothy Parker (1893-1967) was an American short story writer and poet, most fondly remembered for her satirical verse and witty conversation. One of the greatest humorists of her generation, she was a member of a famous group of playwrights, theater critics, newspaper columnists, newspaper and magazine editors, and writers who met regularly for lunch (seated at a large round table) at the Algonquin Hotel in Manhattan.

◆

—MB & PM

With my finger, I scrape the last of the fudge from the bottom of the bowl and lick it off. Instead of scolding me for my poor table manners, my mother watches and waits for me to answer.

"I love it."

She reaches across and gives me a kiss on the cheek and a long, hard hug.

Twenty years later I take my daughter to New York. We browse through Saks Fifth Avenue, FAO Schwartz, and Tiffany's. We eat hot fudge sundaes at Rumplemeyers. She loves the City and dreams of living there when she grows up.

I think of New York as something I can pass on to the grand-children my mother never met—her legacy to me. I took it because it was what she had to give.

Though Rumplemeyers is closed, Hallie Ephron Touger often visits New York City with her husband and two daughters. A freelance writer living near Boston, she recently completed a mystery novel.

✳

When my mother was four months pregnant with Child Number Three, my father was winging his way to America for graduate study in Berkeley. My mother would join my father two years later. We children lived with our grandparents for three years until we emigrated to the United States to join our parents. Jet travel and separation from my immediate family was a fact of my early life.

Fast forward nearly thirty years and I am sitting in a Berkeley cafe with my own family, my one-year-old smearing fruit pulp over his face, and my husband and I having an unprecedented, ugly confrontation with his parents about an upcoming ten-day trip to Ecuador. It was the opportunity of a lifetime: visit Ecuador for a conference, then a vacation sail in the Galapagos afterward. The sticky point: who would watch our son.

Arguing that the separation anxiety of our ten-day absence would emotionally scar their grandson for life, my in-laws vehemently objected to our trip. "But my parents left me and my siblings in the loving care of my grandparents for three years, and I'm not emotionally scarred."

"Yes, you are," said my mother-in-law, shattering a decade-long friend-ship, "you just don't know it."

My husband and I did go on that trip to Ecuador and the Galapagos. My son stayed with his day-care provider on the weekdays and my in-laws watched him after all on the weekend. When we returned home, our son was happy to see us and our lives returned to normal within a week. I looked for signs of emotional scarring, and I can't say I found any.

But then, if you believe my mother-in-law, I'm scarred for life. I'm addicted to travel, to the discovery of other cultures and people. It's become a life-long disease.

I hope my son is so afflicted.

—H. Kuang Chen, "Separation Pangs"

MICHELE G. HANSON

⋆ ⁺ ⋆

Bambini: Reflections in Venice

To conceive or not to conceive,
that is the question.

WE WERE UNAPOLOGETIC TOURISTS IN VENICE, MY HUSBAND
and I, visiting the churches and museums, sneaking a look at souvenirs on vendors' carts, and riding around on the *vaporetti*. We
passed through the Piazza San Marco again and again to admire
the glorious Basilica and listen to music from the cafés. When we
stopped to rest in the public gardens or strolled through the smaller
piazzas, however, we had a glimpse of what it might be like to live
there, and we especially noticed families. On the Riva degli
Schiavoni, the wide pedestrian avenue that fronts the lagoon, couple after couple walked in the early evening with their children
between them, all holding hands. Women doing errands rode
bicycles with a child in a small seat in front of them. Children
helped out in their parents' stores. At restaurant tables, families
shared bread and conversation.

We were completely enamored of this city. What an extraordinary world where cars are not allowed and walking is a given,
where water is the pervasive element. We happily wandered
through narrow streets and over canals, got lost but returned, inevitably, to the Piazza. We started each day by indulging in a caffè
latte, served in individual pitchers of rich dark coffee and creamy

steamed milk. We were charmed by just about everything, from the delivery men who dexterously maneuvered their carts up and down the steps leading to bridges, to the overwhelming Tiepolo fresco on the ceiling of the Chiesa degli Gesuati.

The children charmed us, too. Once, as we ate dinner in an outdoor café, our attention was drawn to a couple and their daughter, who looked about ten. As they walked up the street, the mother pointed out a cat perched on the ledge of a house. "*Lassù, lassù*," her parents said. *Up there*. The girl, laughing, just couldn't see it. Finally her father, in a gesture both natural and tender, laid his hands on either side of her head and pointed her face in the right direction. "*Sì*," she said with satisfaction, "*eccolo*."

Bill and I knew our heads were turned too; we were outsiders, on vacation, but even so, we couldn't help comparing what we saw and imagined of family life here to what we know in the U.S. We don't have a child and have been considering for some time whether to become parents. Our hesitance derives in part from the families we see around us; at the grocery store, for example, where parents yell at their whiny kids. We hear stories from a friend who teaches high school about how disrespectful and even threatening the students are. Television kids are smart-asses, selfish and sneaky.

But from our perspective, Italian children seemed different. More confident, perhaps, less out-of-control. Parents bent down to listen to what their children had to say; their children didn't yell. Teenagers met to talk in the piazzas rather than sit in front of a video game. And so we began to wonder if it might be possible to raise a child with whom we would genuinely like to spend time. Someone we would like to talk, ride trains, and laugh with, someone to whom we could point out cats on ledges, someone for whom we'd enjoy buying gelato after dinner.

We met such a child on our train ride into the city, our first day in Italy. We rushed onto the train just before it pulled out of the station, and easily found seats. Directly across from us was a single woman, a university student with a textbook in her lap, and across the aisle were a woman and her two boys, one about four years old, the other a baby in her arms. As the mother spoke to her chil-

dren we perked up our ears, hoping to eavesdrop unobtrusively
and see how far our small knowledge of Italian would go.

Not very far, as we dis-
covered. But their conversation was clearly colored with
affection and cheer, and
soon the baby was making
eyes at Bill and laughing.
The four-year-old struck up
an animated discussion with
the young woman facing us,
a stranger to him, and eventually the two were singing

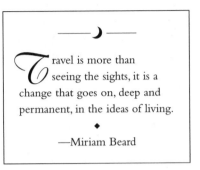

*ravel is more than
seeing the sights, it is a
change that goes on, deep and
permanent, in the ideas of living.*

◆

—Miriam Beard

what must have been advertising jingles. The boy very earnestly
started to describe something he liked a lot: that much we all understood, but even the two women were confused about what he
meant. It had to do with a triangle; he drew the shape in the air.

"Ah," said his mother at last. "*Gli piaciono i cornetti.*"

We all smiled. Of course. He likes to eat his gelato in a cone
rather than a cup.

As the family's station approached, the young woman offered to
take the baby while the mother carried their bags, with my help,
to the door. The mother was very grateful and I completely forgot how to say, "You're welcome." As I returned to my seat, the
young woman was playing spontaneously with the baby.

That image, a woman with a baby in her lap, was one we would
encounter throughout our stay in Venice.

The Virgin Mary appears in every church, larger than life,
impossibly luminous, even though the images hang in the dark
aisles along the side of the nave and the recessed chapels. You can
put coins in a box and an electric spotlight comes on for a couple minutes at a time; you can make a donation and illuminate yet
one more of the many candles that drip before her shrine.
Although she is shown in a variety of scenes—visited by the
Archangel Gabriel (the Annunciation), rising into heaven (the

Assumption), or surrounded by saints—by far the most prevalent and affecting are those where she is holding a baby. A mother and her child. Sensitive as we were to the idea of parenthood, we gazed at these paintings as though to immerse ourselves in their wisdom and beauty. Mary's influence is clearly powerful: we saw old women kneel on hard benches before her, young professionals drop by to worship on their way to work, and tourists stand humbled and transfixed.

She is a fascinating icon. Countless churches around the world are dedicated to her: in France, Gothic cathedrals are known as Notre Dame; in Venice, one of the most notable churches is Santa Maria della Salute; in Florence the imposing Duomo is called Santa Maria del Fiore. And so on. Our Lady of Perpetual Help. Our Lady of Peace, Our Lady of Grace. Her enduring cult speaks to the desire among humans to seek consolation, hope, nurturing and compassion, to whisper into a sympathetic ear.

Something in us perhaps yearns for life's female aspect, *yin,* the mother figure. Scholars make the case that Mary is a version of the archetypal Great Goddess, with roots dating back to ancient cultures. In the medieval church Mary was seen as the defender of humanity against a wrathful God, and even though His image now is not quite so wrought by vengeance and fury, Mary continues to serve as an intercessor, an intermediary. As the archetypal Mother of God, she bridges the human experience and the divine. She is both the humble woman who gave birth in a manger and the woman who, by virtue of the doctrine of the Assumption, became immortal. She concerns herself with our petty trials and yet reigns as Queen of Heaven. In her the mundane and numinous are intertwined.

Although not normally churchgoers, we lit our share of candles.

Our last night in Venice we had an early dinner, walked almost to the public gardens and sat at the edge of the water to enjoy the view. The sun was setting and street lights winked along the Riva. In the distance were the sturdy campanile at San Marco and the gleaming pink-white of the Doges' Palace. Santa Maria della Salute graced the entrance to the Grand Canal, and across the Bacino San Marco floated the silhouette of San Giorgio Maggiore. The lagoon was cast with a metallic blue light, the sky with a pale orange blush. La Serenissima had us in thrall.

Eventually, perhaps inevitably, our conversation turned to the most weighty topic on our minds lately.

"So," said Bill, "should we have a kid?"

We had discussed this often before, revisiting the same hopes and fears, but were unable to resolve them. I took a deep breath and said, "Yes." Intimidated by the import of that answer, however, I qualifyied it. "I think so."

Bill nodded. "How come?"

"We love each other," I said. This is the most compelling reason: we'd like to share that love with a child of our own. We love our families, appreciate their unconditional support for us, the sense of belonging. We believe we would be good and loving parents. These are fine reasons to have a child, and yet....

"But the idea scares me," I admitted. I'm afraid of losing the freedom we have now to travel together, go out for coffee and to movies, take long walks, talk at the breakfast table. A child would change that.

"We could bring her along, couldn't we?" said Bill. This is true: we've seen families traveling together, eating in restaurants, conversing. Even with babies, parents cart around the stroller and diaper bag. They manage. We wouldn't have to give up everything we enjoy; we could compromise and adjust.

"What do you think?" I asked.

"I'd like a child," he said. "Though the world scares me sometimes."

I agreed. Such global problems as war, poverty, crime, and a threatened environment can be depressing enough, but there are also the more personal fears, the potential for sickness and loss, countless small disappointments, cruelty and carelessness, an uncertain future. Such a profound undertaking, to create a new life, nurture her, and still let her be her own person.

Bill looked out at the lagoon, where all sorts of boats were weaving about, even as the light in the sky faded. The air smelled faintly of salt and the water splashed up against the seawall.

"This world can be beautiful, too," he said. And tonight it is, exquisitely so. Not only here, this view. And not only in the churches and museums, where the art and architecture make us catch our breath: the world is beautiful in small moments, too, as when a father wants his daughter to look at a cat, when we feast on perfectly sautéed shrimp, or when we laugh at the grumpy little dog that patrols the Via Garibaldi.

In the Doges' Palace is a painting of Venice, a woman, receiving gifts from Neptune, who pours gold and coins at her feet. Like Neptune, we too are seduced by the city's beauty and are inspired to share our good fortune, to dream recklessly, to live on hope. Another painting, by Veronese, shows "The Triumph (l'Apotheosi) of Venice," where she is a woman floating in the air, receiving a golden crown—not unlike some paintings of Mary surrounded by angels. To me, the personification of Venice is testament to humans' desire to identify with something uplifting, transcendent: what better subject than the very place you inhabit? Surely the Great Goddess is at work here. This is such an improbable city, extraordinary, built on water, always in danger of sinking, they say, but still standing. Centuries-old buildings still shelter its inhabitants, gondolas still ply the canals, and the waiter at the Caffè Paradiso still calls, "Caffè, cappuccino!"

Is it possible to raise a child who is capable of being extraordinary? Are we capable of being so? Here in the mild June evening, with riches all around, we decide.

Yes.

Michele Hanson lives in Buffalo, New York, with her husband, child, and dog. She works as an art librarian and has recently finished a novel about the desert.

★

One year I went to the terrace of the Gritti, the other great hotel on the Grand Canal, to watch the regatta. An old lady wearing a hairnet and white socks and oxfords and a housedress engaged me in conversation about her grandchildren—her gift to the future, she called them—and my children. Children are the good people, she said. When it came time for him to put the tablecloths on the tables, the maitre d' asked me to leave, as I had no reservation. I was sad. The parade of all kinds of vessels, some manned by beautiful young men and women, others by very old hands, is one of the gayest and prettiest sights in the world—everything sparkling and all moods buoyant—and I regretted having to leave the pleasant old lady, too. The pleasant old lady addressed the maitre d' sternly and nodded to me beneficently, and I was allowed to stay and made to feel welcome. When the first gondola pulled up to the Gritti, the gondolier ceremoniously handed the old lady a sheath of roses, addressed her as Contessa, and kissed her hand, as did subsequent boatmen. I never learned the name of the contessa/grand marshal; but this incident—the woman's kindness, the not impersonal negotiations built on the slender thread of mutual affection for the young and on family feeling—enable me to think of Venice in a new and happy way: not as a bazaar or mercantile arena or as a museum, but as a place of shared human responses, a place where people trade in goodness.

—Barbara Grizzuti Harrison, *Italian Days*

MOLLY O'NEILL

* * *

Two for the Road

From morels to motels, a mother and daughter find
more than adventure on the Oregon Trail.

ROUTE 101 WINDS ALONG THE PACIFIC FROM WASHINGTON TO Northern California, twisting and turning through some of America's most electrifying scenery. The jagged coast, with its terrifying rocky drops and tumultuous coves, its peaceful peninsulas and redwood cathedrals, is not unlike the landscape between two people, enmeshed.

Most mother-daughter relationships could profit from a road like 101, which rolls along, negotiating the topography, come what may. Whatever differences my mother and I had before we began our four-day ramble from Seattle to San Francisco, Route 101 kept us together. My mother, you should understand, thinks that weak coffee and soft, warm dinner rolls are the *sine qua non* of fine dining. Knowing this, I was probably less than sensitive in suggesting the Pacific Northwest, land of drive-in espresso stands and artisan bread baking, as the destination for a car trip. But, hey, I was giddy.

As we sped along the Willamette River, past farmlands, vineyards and woods, Oregon's interior exhilarated me. The tidy fields were bordered by blackberry plants and wild greens. Gone was the rain and the mist that shelter the grapes and nurture the wild asparagus and fiddlehead ferns, replaced by a brilliant, unfiltered sun.

Ohio used to be like this, said my mother as she lightly tapped on the imaginary brake she had kept under the passenger seat since I first learned to drive about a million years ago. But nothing about Columbus, Ohio, past or present, compared with the rocky end of the world, where Route 18 reconnected with Route 101. Here, we navigated a perilous passage between thickets of forest and the black hole of eternity. At one point, my mother slammed on her brake and inhaled what she took to be her final breath, and the air whistled through her clenched teeth.

We ate snowy halibut and slabs of sturgeon that night, and later we supped on fresh abalone and Chinook salmon, all otherworldly stuff if your world happens to be central Ohio. I was so relieved not to be driving, I didn't appreciate the low-keyed genius of the food; my mother was so happy to be alive, she didn't question its exoticism. The rare restaurant that served soft dinner rolls pleased her most, though she later conceded, as did I, that we had eaten some of the best meals of our lives on the Oregon Trail. Her continuing loyalty to cheap roadside motels, however, was intimately connected to the character of their free morning coffee, which I had to admit was not so bad. Actually, I had begun to like anything that made my mother happy, which I now think is the way of the world.

The generations learn to accommodate each other by acceding to each other's tastes. The older generation's past goads the younger generation forward. But the motion is always circular. I've been settling for coffee from the corner coffee cart lately, and Mom is sorry to report that fresh sturgeon is not available at the Kroger's on Morse Road.

As we headed into Northern California, with the redwoods beginning to shade our path, we knew something memorable had happened. We noticed how the cars ahead of us occasionally misjudged the turns, and we couldn't help remarking on the dents and gashes flecked with automobile paint on the massive redwood trunks.

Not that any of this made us nervous, for we would reach Eureka and then San Francisco right on time. After all, we'd been down a road like this before.

Molly O'Neill is the food editor for The New York Times.

★

I've given up destination driving. It's the journey that counts. Read the historical markers, take the side road. The unexpected things are often more fun than the grand sights.

—Susan Bistline, *The Fruits of Fifty*

SUSAN WADIA-ELLS

★ ★ ★

The Anil Journals

A mother weaves her adopted son's birth mother into their lives.

I AM ONE-EIGHTH ASIAN INDIAN AND PROUD OF THIS HERITAGE— my curly Parsi hair and intense eyes—and my mother's family, the Wadias, is still one of the most respected Parsi families in India. As a child growing up in Vineland, New Jersey, I had tried to impress my third-grade classmates by speaking "Indian" which I convinced them I was fluent in because my grandmother was half Asian Indian. I also visited India a number of times as a young adult where I often felt as if I had finally come home. Sometimes I could see my grandmother's generous nose, her olive skin and dark penetrating eyes, or the color and texture of my mother's thick hair in the people around me.

I was thirty-nine years old, just married, and unwilling to take any surgical steps to deal with my apparent infertility. I wanted to be a mother, not a medical case. So my life-partner, Larry, and I agreed that we would adopt a child. Larry had never thought about adoption before, let alone the question of where to adopt from. I had always wanted to adopt a child someday. Now that my "someday" had arrived, I wanted to adopt a child from India.

Larry and I applied to the Vermont Children's Aid society, an adoption agency with an ongoing relationship with the large

Calcutta-based International Mission of Hope. The agency said we would most likely receive an infant boy because we were a married couple and most of the many single women applying to adopt children were requesting girls. Soon Larry and I were happily arguing about a name for our forthcoming baby boy.

"He'll need an Indian name," I insisted. "He's Indian, damn it!"

"He's already Indian. He'll need an American name. He's going to live in America," was my partner's retort. For some reason Larry thought that "Alysandyr" sounded American. "We can call him Alex for short," he said.

"Never," I vowed silently to myself. "This child's name is Anil."

Anil, a popular Indian name that means "fresh air" or "wind" in the Hindi language of northern India and "blue sky" in the Bengali language of eastern India, sounded just right to my heart. So in the end, months before any baby was born, we sent off his stack of immigration and adoption papers with a name that was surely longer than the baby himself. "Alysandyr Anil Wadia-Nevin."

A year later when the baby was two months old and legally could be "assigned" to a non-Indian family, we received a note written in English, included in an envelope with our baby's first picture.

"Alysandyr Anil is a handsome little boy as you can see in the photo taken a while back. His nursery name is Anil. It was strange to see that you have also named him Anil."

Who are we to think that we can decide such things as a child's name? I suppose his Bengali nurse and I each chose the name "Anil," not because we liked it better than any other Indian name, but because this was the child's name. Born into a world where his birth mother had to leave him behind, this child, with those eyes that look and smile and miss nothing, knows himself very well. Possibly he is here to teach, more than to learn.

India's largest festival, Diwali, the festival of lights, was just a few days away. Diwali is the happiest holy day of the Hindu calendar and the beginning of India's spiritual year, surely auspicious signs for me as I moved closer and closer toward motherhood.

As the train's ancient coal engine barreled through the north-eastern state of Bihar, all I could think of, looking out at the red tile roofs and glistening black water buffalo wandering near the rice paddies, was that by the end of the day I would have my baby in my arms. I would be a mom.

When the Rajvani Express finally pulled into Calcutta's Howrah Station at 9 a.m., the ragged, cavernous building was teeming with coolies, *sadhus*, mangy dogs, encamped families, fellow travelers, holy cows and soda sellers. At that moment, Calcutta seemed the most beautiful city in the world to me. Larry was not so sure.

A taxi driver saw us—two pink-faced Americans with back-packs—emerge from the station entrance and quickly herded us, along with a tall, middle-aged Indian man with a protruding nose and a faded brown briefcase, into his small, battered Ambassador taxi cab. Packed into the sedan, we lurched forward toward the chaotic mass of traffic slowly moving onto the bridge to down-town Calcutta. It wasn't long before we came to a full stop.

The beak-nosed "professor" lectured us as we sat knee-to-knee waiting for traffic around us to move: "Here in Calcutta, people are all right until they're asked to work. Democracy without edu-cation. In America, time is costly. Here people can wait two hours on a trolley, no problem. In Calcutta, time is the cheapest thing."

Finally, the mass of traffic trembled and our cab began to inch onto India's Golden Gate, the infamous Howrah Bridge, spanning the Hooghly River and carrying passengers between the immense Howrah train station and India's largest city.

"Keep your arm inside. The car can get bumped," the professor barked at me. "This you can see nowhere in the world. Not Bombay, not Delhi, only Calcutta," he continued.

Lines of trolley cars, circa 1940, ran down the middle of the bridge, right alongside our car. People perched on the trolleys' glassless window ledges, dangling their legs in the traffic, while other brave—or foolish—souls squatted on the trolleys' roofs. A few rickshaws, along with bicycles, motor scooters and three-wheeled diesel "phut-phuts," kept trying to squeeze between us and the trolleys. Ahead I could see more black and yellow Am-bassador taxis scattered among huge dump trucks adorned with colorful murals of Hindu gods, landscapes and decorative Bengali script. As we sat in the middle of this Calcutta beehive, the "professor" still venting his frustration with his culture and his fellow countrymen, I smiled, dreaming about my sleeping baby on the other side of town.

When the cab finally inched off the bridge an hour later, we started down a road lined with tall office buildings. Large sections of the pavement were buckled and a broken fire hydrant sprayed gallons of water into the street while skinny children and sharp-boned silver-grey cows waded back and forth in the mud enjoying the festivities. "That's a Calcutta monsoon flood," the professor said, finally drawing some humor from the swirling city scene.

At the hotel, an old British woman behind the reception desk gave me a good map. Tollygunge Circular Road, a short semi-circle of a street, would be a cinch to find. But finding the International Mission of Hope, at 35/6 Tollygunge

---

*O*ver my objections, Iki put my bag in the trunk of their car, a battered Hindustan Ambassador that was unmarked except by mud, no reassuring "Agra Taxi Company" emblazoned on the door. "Thief might steal suitcase in backseat, Madam," Kallu explained. I acquiesced—the dry shelter of the "taxi" looked inviting and I was worn down by the ceaseless demands on my ability to communicate, decipher, make decisions, find, respond, protect, etc., that travel entails, even in a four-star situation, which the Agra train station was decidedly not.

◆

—Pamela Michael,
"The Khan Men of Agra,"
Travelers' Tales: A Woman's World

Circular Road, turned out to be another story. Back and forth we went. The street numbers jumping from 77/8 to 25/6 to 124/5 without notice, around and around, up and down. The driver finally forgot about numbers and started asking for the place for the babies, for IMH, or for what he thought might be the Bengali translation of IMH. On our fourth try down the quiet narrow residential street scattered with stalls selling juice or the spicy betelnut *pan,* sandal fixers, spice merchants and a few small temples, my searching eyes caught a white flash in the sun—a tall, enclosed Jeep, enamel white, with clear black English letters along its side: INTERNATIONAL MISSION OF HOPE.

"It's IMH!!" I screamed as I scrambled out of the taxi and hurried toward a beautiful woman in a blue-and-white-striped cotton sari standing by a door in the heavy sunlight. Larry paid the driver and caught up with me and together we followed the smiling woman into the cool cement building.

No introductions were needed. The nursery staff was waiting for us. We had been sending four-month-old Anil postcards every day telling him we had arrived in India.

Another woman wearing the same IMH cotton sari pointed to a chubby figure sitting on the lap of a woman on the opposite side of the clean, cool room. The nursery was lined wall to wall with sleeping babies in bassinets or held by nurses, while a few larger babies slept peacefully on mats laid in the middle of the floor.

As I began to walk across the still room toward Anil, careful not to trample the sleeping infants, the women holding other babies along the sides of the room began to quietly chant "mother, mother, mother."

Anil knew me immediately as I knelt on the floor and clucked to him. He opened up his big eyes even wider, and a grin broke out on his face.

"That's my Anil," I murmured, as I took him gently and held him close. The tears I had been holding back as I traveled across half of the world's oceans, rivers and roads to reach my son now bathed my face and dripped on his little nose, dissolving us into one big hug.

"That's not our baby," Larry blurted out. "Our baby is not this fat."

The round-faced cherub who now filled my arms stopped smiling and glared at his new father.

"Larry, don't be silly, look at his eyes! He's gained a lot of weight since his picture was taken a few months ago," I whispered

as I too glared at this new father who stood beside me. For many
weeks, while Anil was busy doubling his birthweight, Larry and I
had carried around copies of our one and only photo of Anil, a
skinny two-week-old, six- or seven-pound infant. As new parents,
we would constantly stare adoringly at this picture of our thin-
cheeked baby's face, a face now imprinted in Larry's brain.

During that eventful October day in Calcutta, while my passion remained focused on Anil, my child, I also felt a nagging curiosity about the woman who had given birth to him a few
months earlier. Who was she? How had she become pregnant?
Why had she decided to give up Anil at his birth? What was she
feeling right now about her decision? Would I even be able to
find her, to thank her for this incredible gift? Intellectually I knew
that these questions were probably unanswerable, but without the
ability to thank her, the whole adoption felt somewhat surreal.
How can you have birth without a birth mother?

Before even applying for the adoption, I had been told that the
International Mission of Hope orphanage received babies who had
been abandoned by their birth mothers. These women were
unwed mothers or widows, we were told. It was socially unac-
ceptable for them to even become pregnant. As our adoption papers were processed, IMH had continued to make it stridently
clear that no records of the birth parents would be available for
these children or even existed.

When I asked the IMH director if we might meet the doctor
who had delivered Anil, she suggested that Larry and I accompany
their staff member, Besanti, the next morning as she made her daily
rounds of the "nursing homes." These nursing homes—doctors' offices containing a few hospital beds—are found throughout India.

So the next day, while Anil took his long morning nap at IMH
with his beloved nurse, Kashal-lal, nearby, Larry and I followed
Besanti into a waiting vehicle. On the way, the driver jumped out
at his favorite *pan* stall, hopping back into the black IMH
Ambassador sedan a minute later with two packed banana leaves in
hand. He passed one spicy *pan* to Besanti and offered the other to

Larry, who politely declined. The driver popped the second *pan* in his mouth and, slowly chewing the concoction of red-staining betel nut and spices, moved on into the swirl of downtown Calcutta traffic.

When we stopped by Sri Krishna Nursing Home, where Anil had been born, Besanti and I found Dr. Chakraborty sitting at his desk in the second-floor suite of rooms. First I humbly thanked the tall, grey-haired doctor for delivering my child. Then I asked, "Can you tell me about the mothers who give birth to their babies and then leave them?"

"All of the women who come here are very, very poor," Dr. Chakraborty said in his clipped Indian English. "Some of them have four, five, six children already; they may not even have a home. They cannot keep more children. I am happy though to

*P*an is a mildly intoxicating mixture of betel nuts and spices chewed throughout eastern Asia. Pan sellers are a common sight on city streets, and in many shops and homes you will notice stained remnants of the edible leaf in which it is generally wrapped. Leftovers are usually spit onto the street after extended chewing, leaving little red blotches on the ground. Many people, particularly older ones, will have red stains on their mouths and gums. Remember "Bloody Mary" from *South Pacific*—"Chewing betel nuts?" Why do you think they called her "bloody?"

♦

—MB & PM

give the children to IMH. I have been to your country three times escorting babies. I see how very well cared for these children are. They are quite strong."

Back in the IMH sedan, now stuck in a mid-morning Calcutta traffic jam, Besanti held our first baby of the morning up into the warm sunlight streaming through the car's side window.

"Who are these mothers?" I asked Besanti, as we drove toward yet another nursing home to pick up one or two more waiting newborn babies. Besanti heard my question and gave me a startled look.

"They are not mothers," Besanti said quickly, then lowered her dark eyes and the tiny baby as we moved slowly forward in the line of traffic.

"We rarely see babies who are over three pounds," Cheri Clark, an American nurse and founder of the IMH orphanage, told us later that day. "The doctors who run these little nursing homes used to leave the newborns on the floor until they died. But we have gone round to each of their offices and given them space blankets to cover the children. They know we will come to their offices each day to pick up any babies who have been abandoned. Most of the doctors are using these featherweight insulated blankets now. It's good. Now the babies are alive when we arrive to pick them up."

> The Sanskrit word for mother *(matra)* as well as Greek *(meter)* are also the words for measurement. Thus, mathematics was once called "Mother Wisdom." *Panacea* (all-healer) and *Hygeia* (Health), were the daughters of Mother Rhea Coronis, the Cretan universal mother or Great Goddess of old. Both goddesses are mentioned in the Hippocratic Oath.
>
> ◆
>
> —MB & PM

I nodded mutely, barely hearing her words. There was so much about India I didn't understand.

Tomorrow Larry and I would bundle up Anil, pick up his white canvas IMH bag filled with tiny shirts, sleepers, diapers, wipes and formula and fly west out of Calcutta to Bombay and Vermont beyond. But first Koshal-lal and the other women who had nurtured Anil for the past four months needed to say their good-byes.

"Tell them they are one with the angels," Larry said to Cheri Clark the next day, as Koshal-lal and many of the other *masseys* (Bengali for "mother's elder sister"), stood at the gate waving and wiping tears from their eyes. Larry, his face wet from his own tears, gently carried his son, now sleeping peacefully in his wicker travel basket, into the waiting Ambassador cab. Our grey-bearded Sikh driver, tall in his red turban, stood holding the door while I snapped pictures of everyone in sight. We were all part of Anil's ongoing birth story, his second or third delivery of sorts, I figured. Looking at my calm, sleeping baby, I suddenly wondered how many lives this child had already had....

From the first photo taken a few weeks after his birth, to our present-day life, Anil has seemed the "old soul" of the three of us. His eyes have always been deep and centered. Never a wild-eyed innocent baby, he has always had a knowing sense about him. Even today at the ripe old age of eight he will sit, looking out at the mountains, stroking his dog, lost in his thoughts for long periods of time.

"How long did it take you to get to India?" he asked me one night recently as we were nuggling down to go to sleep.

"You were nineteen weeks old when we arrived in Calcutta."

"What did my birth mom say to Koshal-lal when she gave me to her?" I realized that it was time to revise Anil's birth fable. "I don't know, but I would love to know," I said. "If I could get to meet your birth mom, I would be so excited and so happy to see her that I would make a mess. I would start to cry and cry and cry and say, 'Thank you. Thank you for giving me Anil to be my baby, because I am lucky to have the bestest baby in the whole world.'"

And Anil said, "No, Mom, you can't say those things. Don't say so: don't brag. How much did I weigh when you got me?" he asked, quickly changing the subject.

"Twelve pounds," I said. "You were one of the biggest babies who ever lived at IMH. You were already six pounds when you were born."

"Is my birthday the same day that you and Daddy met me in Calcutta?"

"No," I said. "you were born on June 18 and we got to Calcutta October 28, just before Halloween. Should we celebrate that day?"

"Yes," he said adamantly.

"We'll call it our family birthday, because that's the day we all became a family," I said. "We'll each have two birthdays. That will be nice."

"Yeah," he said, before drifting off to sleep.

Longtime educator, feminist, and activist Susan Wadia-Ells wrote this story for her anthology, The Adoption Reader: Birth Mothers, Adoptive Mothers and Adopted Daughters Tell Their Stories. *She lives in Vermont with her son, Anil.*

★

Mimi was with her birthmother, Chandra Maya, for the first fourteen months of her life, until we adopted each other. It was definitely not a one-way process. She lost her father before she was even born, and Chandra struggled in her carpet weaving job to support Mimi, her two sisters, and one brother.

Chandra ran away from home at fourteen, I think because she feared being sold into prostitution and sent to a Bombay brothel. She went to Kathmandu and became a weaver in a Tibetan carpet factory. She was paid by the piece. It would take her about 40 hours to weave a square meter of carpet, for which she was paid a few dollars. The family lived in a room, just big enough for two small beds, a kerosene cook stove, and a couple of shelves. They owned a few blankets, a few pots, and a few pieces of clothing. Nothing more. The water pump and squat toilet shed in the factory compound were shared by all the residents, about 75 people, mostly children.

This past summer, Chandra was diagnosed with tuberculosis and, although she is expected to recover, is now unable to work or care for her other children. Fortunately, a sponsor has been found for them, so they're boarding at a school in Kathmandu. The factory community in which she was living shunned her for giving up Mimi for adoption and she has had to move.

Chandra Maya has suffered so many losses in her twenty-six years— her village life, husband, children, health, community of support, and means of survival. But she hasn't lost her captivating, serene beauty, or her quick, though unschooled, intelligence. And I tell her that she hasn't lost her daughter. We are sharing her, as *bahini* and *didi* (little sister and big sister). I've been blessed with a remarkable daughter, a once-in-a-lifetime week of spending time Nepali-style on the roof with my daughter's birth family and friends, and now an extended family back in Nepal. I know that we'll go back often to spend time getting to know them better.

—Ellie Skeele, "Bahini and Didi"

STEPHANIE LEVIN-GERVASI

* ✳ *

Lessons of the Rainforest

Entrusting your child to a stranger
is one of the hardest things to do.

I WAS WARNED BY FEMININE SAGES THAT MOTHERHOOD WOULD impinge upon my free spirit. Undeterred and a few bottles of Clomid later, I was pregnant at age 42. Camille arrived six weeks premature while I was on a writing assignment in the California wine country. Motherhood curtailed my travel writing; it did not extinguish my wanderlust. I straddled two worlds, one of diapers, the other of dreams. I loved my daughter, but longed to slip into the unknown, bask in sensuous breezes and sultry downpours in exotic destinations. I envied friends who traveled afar and placed my maternal faith in time and genes.

When an invitation to join a family cruise to Costa Rica materialized, I said "*si*," and put on a *cumbia* to sashay around the living room. The celebration was short lived. My husband announced he couldn't go, business in the Big Apple.

I thought about canceling, convinced that I couldn't keep track of my daughter and write a story in the same breath. I adjusted my attitude and booked reservations for two. Immediately, the soothsayers, called full of perilous, portentous news—hurricanes, heat rashes, and rum addictions. Hike the rainforest with my four-year-old in tow; had my fortyish neurons gone awry, questioned an ex-friend. The litany didn't unravel my resolve.

At the exact moment the Rain Gods angrily spit on the Caribbean, my daughter and I landed in San Jose, Costa Rica.

I'd spend my 20s and 30s on Spanish soil ambling from Madrid to Mar de Plata, culminating with a marriage to an Argentine. I'm fond of Latino airport order, it's refreshingly chaotic, freeing—one line, ten thousand suitcases coiled in straps, and gray panthers pushing to the head of the line. Camille sprinted about the maze, conversing with strangers. Even in the confines of this small Central American airport, I knew she had innocently happened upon the wellspring of her existence—the freedom to be a child. *Gracias á Dios,* it was contagious.

We bound willy-nilly through the capital in a mini-bus, seat-belts unhooked, windows down, giggling like loons. Our hotel, Grano de Oro, was a sweet little replica out of *One Hundred Years of Solitude*—lush gardens and a rich sense of poetic justice. Eldon and Laura Cook, two expatriate Canadians, greeted us. They had three daughters and, in my book, big hearts. We settled on the patio and the kids flitted amidst tables, bougainvillea, and jutting ginger. No one batted an eye, so I drank one more guava concoction before bed.

I had chosen the most comfortable access to the most out of the way places. The cruise ship, a 63-passenger, 173-foot boat boasting eco-sensitive stops, was our home for the next ten days. Our crew was under thirty, unpretentious, and knowledgeable. We met the rest of the passengers over a life-saving drill, a thrill that sent Camille spinning around the stern. She spotted three bigger boys, not one interested in playing with a girl. I realized Camille was the only little girl onboard and obviously too small to hike the moun-tainous terrain. I sniffed a soothsaying spirit onboard.

"Who will take care of Camille while I hike?" I asked the Captain in charge.

"At your service," said José, a 26-year-old, dark-eyed beauty of a man who made me blush when he smiled.

"José," I worried aloud, picturing my little girl wandering

around the boat in her swimsuit with this six-foot man. "Camille doesn't swim and she doesn't sit still and she understands Spanish," I warned.

"Don't worry, this is Costa Rica, not California," came the polite admonishment.

I went to bed a little worried. At dawn I roused Camille's sleepy body, dressed her, and carted her upstairs to José. Then, I wondered if I'd lost touch with reality.

We took a dinghy to shore, and Camille took José's hand and bid me good-bye as the two strolled off into the dawn. Was Captain José a *curandero* who had cast some spell over my daughter? Two days in the tropics and not even a good-bye kiss for mama.

I followed my fellow travelers. The verdant village swallowed us. Fresh rainwater poured from vines and delicate orchids pursed their petals. Exotic creatures screeched, insisting the guide raise his nearly inaudible voice. He tells us everything is here, if we know where to look. An allspice tree to cure influenza, a monkey-ear tree to build canoes, gumbo-limbo to treat skin rashes—the planet's perfect ecosystem.

I ease up the muddy trail behind my guide. Tony is a Tica in his late 20s, short, dark hair, fair skin. He tells me his son is three, a year younger than my daughter. And he brings his child to the forest, just as his grandfather had brought him, and taught him how to use plants, what to touch, what to avoid.

"Red," he warns, "in the rainforest is dangerous. Red plants are poisonous, red animals too." Tony is not a man of many words, but I steer clear of rainforest red, vowing to warn my daughter to leave her favorite color alone.

Cradled by ancient deciduous forest and medicinal mysteries, I'm humbled. I close my eyes, see indigenous mothers plucking salve to tend a child's wounds. The trees have spirits, wisdom; I feel their breath, their strength.

"They are interdependent," continues Tony, "all epiphytes or flora support on one another for survival."

Tony is talking about the strangler fig, its tendrils fused together to create a crude mesh. Suddenly, a rare childish instinct overrides common sense. I wind my way through the giant knotted tendril roots and branches growing helter-skelter. I'm trying to digest the lecture on how the fig develops a crown of leaves, shades and strangles its host when I notice an army of ants marching across my foot. The column wolf packs by the thousands with one intent— turn my toes into skeletons.

I envisioned the headlines back home—"Mother devoured by fastidious foragers, daughter lost in the jungle." I leapt off the fig tendrils and checked my watch. I needed to get back to the beach.

On the sand I notice two busy shadows in the distance.

"Hi mom, did you have a good hike?" yelled Camille as she waved me past with her sand bucket and headed toward José.

Surprised, I watched the Captain and my daughter fill the sea with sand. The stretch of beach was her unrestricted palace, free of restrictions. The rules were simple here—don't feed the *agouties* or touch red.

"So what did you two do all morning?" I asked.

Camille pointed to brown-nose pelicans, and mentioned a few white face monkeys. "The monkeys are nice, but the beach is better. And I wanted to bring you back a coconut but José said if I picked the coconuts no trees would grow in their places. Sorry mama, no coconuts, only trees. And please remember something else. You need to treat the earth well. It was not given to you by your parents, it was loaned to you by your children."

I thanked José for the ecology lesson and taking care of Camille. His kindness had given me the opportunity to experience the marvels of the splendid tropical canopy. I told him I'd come

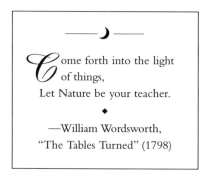

Come forth into the light of things,
Let Nature be your teacher.

◆

—William Wordsworth,
"The Tables Turned" (1798)

to Costa Rica with a deep longing, to rejuvenate my sluggish soul, laugh, lighten up, and splash in the sea with my daughter. But something else had happened. The rich tableau of tropical influences had forever altered the way I looked at the world. Surrounded by Costa Rica's fenceless zoo, I felt compelled to save poisonous frogs, sea turtles, green iguanas, and tropical forests, to leave some small legacy of the earth intact for my daughter's generation.

Camille's goal was not so noble. She combed the beaches under cloudless skies, and interacted with bugs and strange people. There were a hundred watchful eyes protecting every one child; she felt safe. It seemed so natural, so out of time with our urban routine. How liberating to be in a country that loved children, didn't silence their curiosity, or rein in their spirits. One minute Camille was an iridescent blue Morpho in Corcovado, the next an magnificent Quetzal in Golfito. She skirted about, her little being saying, "Fly mama, fly, no one clips your wings here."

At night we stretched, two lazy lizards on the deck. I drank rum, Camille had Shirley Temples. Geraldo, the bartender, invited Camille behind the open bar to concoct her own Shirleys, a scandalous act in the States, a perfectly natural gesture in Central America. Geraldo put on the *Macarena* and transformed the deck into a floating dance hall; time suspended beneath the galaxy and the sea. The salt-drenched air perfumed the night. And well past *medianoche,* Camille and I crawled into our bunks, opened the port windows, followed moon shadows, and counted the constellations. I loved her more than I thought possible to love another human being, her innocence, her trust in coconuts and people. I knew in her young worldly way she was asking me to do the same, to trust my heart.

Our last day was spent on Cano Island. I hiked and Camille guarded the beach. By now, a few other Costa Rican children had joined the cruise and the entire crew stayed on the beach with the kids. My last hike into the rainforest was humid, sticky, and familiar. I descended the muddy forest deep in conversation with the guide. Screams sailed across the silent sky. My throat tightened and my legs turned to noodles. Even before I smelled the sea, I felt Camille's screams. I darted from the group and grabbed her little body huddled on the ground.

"It's a bee sting, and she's very upset," said a crew member close to tears.

Camille had never been stung by a bee before and memories of my friend Stan Barr, who died from a bee sting in his backyard, panicked me. Nadir, a biologist, apparently read my morbid thought.

"She doesn't have an allergic reaction, she's just frightened," he reassured me.

"I feel like the worst mother on earth, plotting about saving the rainforest, and I couldn't save my daughter if I had to," I blubbered through tears.

"You're in God's pharmacy, all his medicinal secrets grow here, even remedies for bee stings. But you know, the best remedy to pull that little sucker of a stinger out is urine," said Nadir.

"Pee!" stuttered Camille, jumping to her feet. "You're not going to pee on my neck, are you Mama? I feel better already."

"Me too," I said. "Let's go hug a tree, take a swim, and head back to the ship for a Shirley Temple."

Stephanie Levin-Gervasi wanted to see the entire world before her thirtieth birthday. She didn't, but managed to spend the better part of two decades living in Spain, Mexico, and France. She considers herself a passionate Franco/Latinophile and has kept journals of her travels since 1975. Her numerous encounters with ancient cobblestone corners and indigenous spirits has forever changed her perception of the world, but so did having a child at age 43.

★

Last spring, I saw a student on campus in a t-shirt that said, "Love Your Mother," and showed an astronaut's photo of the cloud-splashed Earth. To be honest, the t-shirt irritated me, and so did the student. I wondered if he ever wrote to his mother or remembered her birthday. I wondered if the student had figured out what it means to think of the Earth as a mother: Mother Earth, Magna Mater. I wondered if he had ever thought about it, if he had any idea how complicated the analogy is—in what particular way—we are supposed to understand the connection between the Earth and a mother, and what a difference that connection makes for the way we live, what obligations it imposes.

Maybe he's pointing out that the Earth, like a mother, is productive, reproductive, and that we humans are born of the earth, just as the Earth is born of star-matter spinning in long spirals from the explosion of the Big Bang. But what difference does that relationship make? Humans may be made of earth-matter, but so are Oldsmobiles, and that doesn't make the Earth into the Mother of Oldsmobiles, and it doesn't explain the source of our obligations.

—Kathleen Dean Moore, *Riverwalking: Reflections on Moving Water*

* * *

The Guilt Trip

Learning to shed extra baggage
is a mother's dilemma.

MY WORK REQUIRES ME TO TRAVEL FREQUENTLY AND OFTEN FOR extended periods, making me even more vulnerable to self doubt than the average working or traveling mother. Subtle criticism from several non-working moms in my community about my occasional one- or two-week absences has hit me hard at times. Still worse, I love what I do! Combined, all of the above led me at one point to question almost everything about my role as a parent. Was I a good mother? A good enough mother? Was my babysitter the best available? Did my husband resent the extra work at home while I was away? With every trip, I packed and hauled along such awful extra baggage. Shouldered every mile, along with my duffels, totes, and briefcase, I dragged this heavy load of doubt and reproach. The quiet claws of uncertainty became a constant part of my planning, packing, and leave-taking for years. The pain of separation and concern about my family's well-being clouded the joy of taking off for those new worlds I was supposed to be exploring.

Often my flights would leave very early in the morning. I would tiptoe into my children's bedroom to say my silent good-byes while they were still fast asleep, inhaling the familiar fragrance of shampoo in their silken hair, nuzzling my nose into their soft, warm necks, and running my fingers over their downy cheeks. Then I would burst into tears on the way to the airport.

The intensity of my goodbyes varied with every trip. I learned that leaving a sick child or being absent for more than one weekend took the heaviest emotional toll. I suffered one of my worst bouts of guilt when my daughters were three and six years old and I went to Morocco for seventeen days on business—the longest I had ever been away from home. But, it was that very trip that ultimately freed me and put my life back into perspective.

For weeks before my departure for North Africa I took extra precautions to keep every microbe away from my children. Compulsively I spent every free moment playing with them. I made endless lists and schedules for my husband and the babysitter, stocked the cupboards and refrigerator to overflowing, and filled "goodie bags" with simple, gift-wrapped treats to be opened each day I was away. But even my best efforts didn't alleviate my guilt.

Although the pain of separation faded slowly with the excitement of experiencing Africa, I still felt stabs of guilt each day. To comfort myself and stay emotionally connected to home I carried pictures of my family with me everywhere and enthusiastically shared them with waitresses, guides, and travel companions. I safety-pinned my favorite snapshots to the canvas walls of my tent when camping in the Sahara Desert. One day I pulled them out of my backpack to share with a nomadic Bedouin woman and her newborn baby as she boiled water for tea over a wood fire. Together we smiled and cooed over her child and my pictures.

In Marrakesh, I placed a framed picture of my daughters on the bedside table in my hotel room, as had become my custom. For years I had performed the same nesting ritual in every new hotel, in every city: I would throw open the curtains for light, mess up the covers on the bed, and ceremoniously place framed snapshots of my children and husband all over the room. Perched on the nightstand, inches from my head, the smiles of my daughters would soothe me as I fell asleep.

I thought of them constantly, and shopping for treasures to take home filled the small amount of free time I had on my first day in the city. In the bustling, colorful alleys of the medina I bargained for tiny embroidered slippers with turned-up toes, leather camels, and exotic dolls. Finally, exhausted from the noonday heat, I returned to the oasis of my hotel room, eager for a few minutes of silence and a cool shower. But, when I unlocked the door I immediately smelled flowers. In a moment I saw them. There, around the picture of my children, fragrant roses had been arranged, transforming the bedside table into a beautiful altar with offerings. But from whom? This touching but mysterious ritual continued for two days. Magically, fresh flowers kept appearing to adorn my children's smiles.

On my last day in Morocco I returned to the hotel late in the afternoon. As I stepped out of the elevator, I heard a rustling in the hall. A short woman with flashing brown eyes and a charcoal-colored bun quickly pushed aside her maid's cart and hurried to greet me. She had obviously been waiting for this moment. Motioning me closer with her keys, she unlocked my door. As I followed her into the room I was once again struck by the sweet smell of flowers. The new offerings were red, white, and pink carnations.

The woman led me to the bedside table where she lovingly lifted the picture of my daughters to her chest and held it tightly. Then she raised the frame to her lips and kissed each girl's photo. I pointed to the flowers, bowed my head, and tried to express my thanks with my hands pressed together in the universal gesture of prayer. Smiling, the woman then pulled a crumpled photograph of her own family from her apron pocket. I took it, admired her four children, then held the picture to my chest and embraced it as she had, gently kissing each child. I reached out to touch her arm in appreciation, and she hugged me closely. As we stood embracing in silent female communion, tears filled my eyes and my throat choked closed with emotion.

Using only gestures and our eyes and smiles, we told each other about our children, and I felt blessed and quietly at peace. This was the true reward of travel: not the places visited but the people who have touched my life. This compassionate Muslim woman reminded me once again that mothers all over the world work, often outside the home, and are thus separated from their children by that work. It is not a choice for most of them, or for most of us. And we are not bad mothers because of it.

In that brief moment of sharing family pictures in a strange city so far from home, I realized that nothing has ever made me as happy or as sad as Motherhood. And that nothing has ever been quite as hard, as intense, or as satisfying.

Occasionally in my travels I experience something that forever alters my life, that brings me back a changed person. So it was in a quiet room in Marrakesh. Despite my homesickness, a generous Moroccan mother helped me replace guilt with gratitude forever.

Marybeth Bond is the author of Gutsy Women *and* Gutsy Mamas *and the editor of* Travelers' Tales: A Woman's World, *which won a Lowell Thomas Gold Award for best travel book. She traveled alone around the world at age 29. In all, the guilt-free global journey took her two years. Since then, she has included in her life a husband, two young children, a dog, and dozens of pampered rose bushes.*

*

Hawaii was perfect in all the usual ways. The trouble came with the telephone call, the ranch, the food, the policeman. Mostly it was the telephone call.

I'd been on the road for more than two weeks at that point, first in New Zealand, then in Australia, and now in Hawaii. I'd been wowed by rain forests, red sand, and burning lava. But then I spent a morning at a ranch that had been the largest in America owned by an individual, but he'd died and it wasn't the largest any more, and besides the ranch "experience" consisted of museums and houses instead of steers and horses. Afterward, my only bad meal of the trip had left me feeling queasy. And then when I called home my six-year-old son said, "Mom, you've been gone so long I don't remember what you look like."

Just put a dagger in my heart and twist it.

On the way down the hill to the airport, I was stopped by a policeman for speeding. By the time the airplane to Honolulu took off, I had turned face to the window and started to cry. The next day was better. Hawaii is still wonderful. My son still loves me. And I hope I never have a day worse than that.

—Katherine Calos, "The Phone Call"

MARY CATHERINE BATESON

⋆ ⁎ ⋆

Improvisation in a
Persian Garden

*An anthropologist takes her daughter
into the field.*

WE BEGIN IN A PERSIAN GARDEN. IN SUMMER IT WOULD BE FILLED
with scent and color, but on this midwinter day, only the bones of
the garden and its geometries were visible: a classic walled garden,
with ranks of leafless fruit trees between patches of dirty snow and
rosebushes recognizable by their thorns. There was a row of dark
cypresses along one end and a dry watercourse down the center,
clogged with leaves.

I had arrived in Teheran with my husband, Barkev, and our
two-and-a-half-year-old daughter, Sevanne, known as Vanni, for
the beginning of a period of research, teaching and institution
building in a culture and language new to both of us, even though
I had studied the Islamic tradition in the Arab world and Barkev
had grown up as an Armenian Christian in Aleppo, Syria. The day
before, we had gone to tea—in fact, cocktails—at the home of our
new landlords, and when they heard that I was an anthropologist,
they invited us to come with them the next day to a garden on
family land in a village near Teheran, where they would observe
Eyd-e Qorban, the Feast of Sacrifice.

At the same time that pilgrims are performing the Meccan pil-
grimage, Muslims around the world are celebrating some of the

steps of that weeklong ritual, one of which is an animal sacrifice, usually a sheep or a camel. It is said that in Saudi Arabia so many sheep and camels are slaughtered by pilgrims that they are simply plowed under by bulldozers. Many families in Iran also sacrifice a sheep on the Feast of Sacrifice, and here the meat is traditionally given to the poor. When our landlady invited us, although Barkev could not come, well, of course I said I would, but I would have to bring Vanni with me.

On the way to the country, I began to have second thoughts and found myself running a mental race with the car, trying to work out the implications of the invitation I had lightheartedly accepted: to come and see a sheep being slaughtered, bringing a two-year-old child. I worried about what to say to her, how she would react. I went back over the memory of seeing the necks of chickens wrung when I was a child, before chickens came reliably headless, neatly butchered, and wrapped in plastic on little non-biodegradable white trays. Those who eat meat, I told myself, should at least know where it comes from. That trip to Iran was not the first time I had entered a strange culture, but this was the first time I had done so with a child, and this was the first of many moments when the double identity of mother and field-worker led me down new paths of reflection.

I know now that to be in such a garden was to stand in the middle of a vision of the world. In the Persian tradition, a garden is itself a cosmological statement, a diagram reiterated in the design of carpets and the way they are used. Gardens are generally symmetrical in plan, but within that ordered framework the rich particularity is varied and relaxed. Gardens are bounded, walled: within, all is fertile and hospitable, but there is always an awareness of a world outside that is less benign, an unruly and formless realm of desert harshness and marauding strangers.

Water is a part of every garden, either flowing or a pool large enough for the ritual washing that precedes prayer. House agents used to point out the pools to Westerners as wading pools for their children, but in fact these pools, reflecting and doubling garden and sky, focus the ideals of purity and generosity. The Shah built a palace in the northern part of Teheran, at the high edge of the city, so water from the palace garden would symbolically flow down through the city to his subjects. Every garden is a promise of the paradise to which the faithful will go after death.

It was a cold, gray day, and all of us were bundled up. My hostess, elegant in a fur coat and stylish boots, explained that the butchering would be done by the gardener. She herself, she said, could never bear to look on at the moment the sheep was killed. When we arrived we found the gardener and his whole family waiting: his wife, wearing the dark printed cotton veil of a village woman, and three children of different ages. Our gathering modeled the tensions of Iranian society before the revolution: the affluent, Westernized urbanites, the villagers, the performance of a ritual that rooted all of them in the past—all this in a setting with its own affirmations about the relationships between God and humankind and the nature of the cosmos.

The sacrifice of a sheep links several religious traditions. The Patriarch Abraham, we are told, was commanded by God to sacrifice his son—Ishmael in the Islamic version, Isaac for Jews and Christians; then, at the last moment, he was provided with a ram as a substitute.

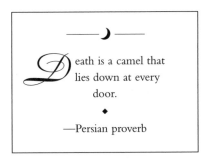

*D*eath is a camel that lies down at every door.

♦

—Persian proverb

The story is emphasized most in Islam, representing the value of total submission to the will of God, a God who proves compassionate. Volumes have been written about the relationship between this single observance and older traditions of human and animal sacrifice and their echoes in Jewish, Christian and Islamic worship. In the rituals of Passover and Easter, the recurrent sacrifice is reshaped in various ways: the shank of bone of a lamb on the Seder table, the Lamb of God imaged in the single atoning sacrifice of

Good Friday and its year-round memorials. There in that garden an ancient symbol connecting many faiths was still a real sheep that would bleed real blood.

The sheep was given a drink of water and turned toward the south, toward Mecca. Then, saying "in the name of God," and "Allahu Akbar," the gardener quickly slit its throat, letting the blood gush out into a ditch. I was holding Vanni on my hip and explaining what was happening, for children can handle such scenes (including those we see every day on television) if they see them in the company of an adult who both interprets and sets an emotional tone.

The sheep was skinned and its various organs removed. The gardener made a slit above one hind hoof and began to blow into it, forcing air under the skin to separate it from the flesh, so the body gradually puffed out and he could slit down the front and re-move the woolly pelt. Deftly he spread the fleece, wool side down, on the ground, to receive the various edible organs, one by one. "See, Vanni," I said, "that's a heart; every animal has one. Its job is pushing the blood around the body all the time." I wondered if I should introduce the word *pump*? No time. Intestines, stomach, liver...some were harder than others to explain, and my mind was racing for vocabulary to convey an understanding of the similarity of all mammals that would not trigger too much identification with the dead sheep. The fleece and the organs neatly laid out upon it would be the butcher's portion.

I had slipped into a teaching role, taking advantage of the visual aids to give a minilecture about each organ, using a vocabulary ap-propriate to a verbal two-and-a-half-year-old. Then suddenly, just as I was saying, "That big thing is a lung, see, for pulling in air and breathing, and the sheep has two of them, just like we do—here comes the other." I thought, with a moment of intense shock, Why, it's huge. In fact, I had never observed the death or dissection of any mammal larger than a mouse. Because I had an abstract knowledge of anatomy, distanced from the reality, and because I was preoccupied with Vanni's experience, it was almost impossible to realize that I was encountering something new myself. What I was passing on to her was not knowledge based on direct experience but a set of labels, whose theoretical character was invisible to me until I was jolted by a detail I had failed to anticipate. My words could hardly have been more abstract if I had started from theological or Biblical history.

Just as I could say, *That's a heart, that's a lung*, we go through life saying, *I must be in love. Oh, this is seasickness, This is an orgasm, This is midlife crisis.* We are ready with culturally contracted labels long before we encounter the realities, even to the point of saying, *This is a heart attack, I must be dying.* We can call our fate by name before we meet it. It will not retreat, but we are often relieved when doctors name our conditions.

The facts of the body both separate and connect. They testify to the links between human beings and other mammals and living systems, but they divide the sexes and the developmental stages. The body's truths are often concealed, so it is not always easy to learn about birth or sex or death, or the curious and paradoxical relationships between them. We keep them separate and learn about them on different tracks, just as we learn separately about economics and medicine and art, and only peripheral vision brings them back together. Experience is structured in advance by stereotypes and idealizations, blurred by caricatures and diagrams.

In the past, we might have climbed as children onto a big fourposter used in turn for birthing, lovemaking, and dying. In other cultures we might have grown up seeing human bodies of every age: torsos as distinctive as faces; breasts of many forms and stages, from the barely budding to the flat, long breasts of multiple lactations; penises as varied as noses. Living in a palm and bamboo hut or under a roof without surrounding walls, we would have listened at night to the sounds people make when their bodies are busy with the primordial efforts of pain or pleasure. We might have seen the interiors of human bodies as well, in places where custom demands the dismemberment of the newly dead. In the modern West, however, even intimacy is categorized and filtered through abstractions.

Anthropologists are trained to be participants and observers at the same time, but the balance fluctuates. Sometimes a dissonance will break through and pull you into an intense involvement in an experience you had distanced by thinking of yourself as coolly looking on. Or it may push you away when you have begun to feel truly a part of what is happening. I was in that garden as a learner, an outsider, and yet, because I was there as a parent, I was simultaneously a teacher; an authority. Trying to understand and remember what I saw, I was also trying to establish an interpretation that would be appropriate for Vanni, one that would increase her understanding of the living world and her place in it and also bring her closer to the Iranians she would be living among for several years. At least, I wanted to leave her unfrightened. Out of that intense multiplicity of vision came the possibility for insight.

That day in the Persian garden has come to represent for me a changed awareness of learning pervading other activities. Meeting as strangers, we join in common occasions, making up our multiple roles as we go along—young and old, male and female, teacher and parent and lover—with all of science and history present in shadow form, partly illustrating and partly obscuring what is there to be learned. Mostly we are unaware of creating anything new, yet both perception and action are necessarily creative. Much of modern life is organized to avoid the awareness of the fine threads of novelty connecting learned behaviors with acknowledged spontaneity. We are largely unaware of speaking, as we all do, sentences never spoken before, unaware of choreographing the acts of dressing and sitting and entering a room as depictions of self, of resculpting memory into an appropriate past.

This awareness is newly necessary today. Men and women confronting change are never fully prepared for the demands of the moment, but they are strengthened to meet uncertainty if they can claim a history of improvisation and a habit of reflection. Sometimes the encounter takes place on journeys and distant sojourns, as it has for me in periods of living in Israel, the Philippines, and Iran. Often enough we encounter the strange on familiar territory, midway through familiar actions and commitments, as did the Iranian gardener whose cosmopolitan employers had become half foreign to him. Sometimes change is directly visible, but sometimes it is apparent only to peripheral vision, altering the meaning of the foreground.

What I tried to do that day, stringing together elements of previous knowledge, attending to catch every possible cue, and exploring different translations of the familiar, was improvise responsibly and with love. Newly arrived in Iran, I had no way of knowing what was going to happen, not even a clear sense of my own ignorance. Even so, I was trying to put together a way of acting toward my child and my hosts that would allow all of us, in courtesy and goodwill, to sustain a joint performance.

Vanni of course was generating a novel performance too, trying to figure out who to be and how to react, the complex perennial task of childhood. She got some of her cues from me, but she also kept a watchful eye on the children of the gardener: the oldest who watched as he had many times before, with a sense of occasion and none of horror, and the younger ones gleaning the confidence that this was an ordinary, unfrightening process taking place in front of them, but a solemn and even festive moment as well, one that would be repeated and explored in play.

So there we were, nine people differing in at least four dimensions: adults and children, females and males, Iranians and Americans, affluent urbanites and villagers, with differences of language and religion falling along the same cleavages. We were joined in the performance of a ritual, in spite of the fact that we did not share a common script or common doctrines. What was happening had different meanings to each of us. The contrasts were as great between the sophisticated urban people and the villagers, who were all nominally Muslims and Iranians, as between the American outsiders and our hosts. Men and women, nominally sharing the same culture, must bridge comparable gaps, yet for better or worse they have always done so, for all human beings live with strangers.

Mary Catherine Bateson is a professor of anthropology and English at George Mason University. She received her undergraduate degree from Radcliffe and a Ph.D. from Harvard University. Her many books include

With a Daughter's Eye, Our Own Metaphor, Composing a Life, *and* Peripheral Visions: Learning Along the Way, *from which this story was excerpted. She is the daughter of Margaret Mead and Gregory Bateson.*

★

Abdul Kalich lives in his mother-in-law's house, across the lane from the river, behind a willow fence, through a gate, and into a mud courtyard shared with a cow, a goat, and chickens. When we arrive, it is twilight and a clap of hands dispatches someone to spread out a carpet in front of the house. Over this is laid a quilt and, on top of the quilt, one pillow. I am motioned toward it, and Abdul comes to sit beside me. Another handclap brings his seven-year-old son with the *hookah* water pipe for his father.

After a while, his mother-in-law comes to sit beside me. From the out-door kitchen, we are served spicy tea and *nan* bread. Then, one by one, the women of the house take turns coming to sit with me. Nura could be Abdul's older sister, she has the same face. She is five months pregnant and carrying a feverish two-year-old on her hip. I meet an "adopted" daughter and many cousins, some of the thirteen people who sleep in the four rooms of the house.

To cover what I take as awkward silences, I attempt woman-talk, prais-ing Abdul's omelets, asking questions. But my hosts have no such com-pulsions. Mostly, we sit in what Kipling calls the "uncounted Eastern min-utes," watching night fall on the river. Snatches of conversation echo through the courtyard and interrupt the wheeze of the *hookah*. Abdul inhales deeply, anxiously cradling his pale daughter as we settle into the muggy darkness together, whacking away at the first mosquitoes.

—Virginia Barton Brownback, "Into the Heart of Kashmir,"
San Francisco Examiner

DENISE M. SPRANGER

✦ ✦ ✦

The Swimming Lesson

The author deepens her relationship
with her companion's son.

THE BRIGHT YELLOW TRIANGLES OF RUBBER FINS DANGLED LOOSELY
from his hand. The strap of his mask trapped wisps of blonde hair
above the snorkel hanging from his left ear; it knocked into his
cheek with the rhythm of our steps down the sidewalk. Just at the
end of the lawn and across the street were the impossibly turquoise
waters of the Mexican Caribbean. As we trudged through the
salted heat of island summer, they glimmered, tempting as a mirage. Uriah, at nine, kept several strides ahead of us. It seemed that
the sea had cast a line and hooked him to it. Teresa and I tried to
quicken our pace as the intensity of blue reeled him in.

It was the first time that this boy of the desert would know the
freedom of a tropical ocean. Until now, his brief encounters with
the sea were of rolled pants legs and hurried feet as he splashed
with his grandfather on Oregon shores. Here, no thunder of surf
would darken the sky-blue waters; no flash of cold, no swirling
tides would warn him of foreboding dangers. Today, at last, the
ocean was his. By the way his sandals slapped the pavement in an
eager march, I could already tell that he knew it.

Yet I worried a little. This is why I wore not one mask, but
two. One was the clear lens pushed up on my forehead. The

97

other, merely the adult attempt to cloak anxiety with a glaze of excitement. The opaque blue that stretched before us was not a swimming pool. There were no numbers painted in black, marking depth on concrete edges. No orange rings, like huge candy life savers, would stand sentinel on steaming walls. I wondered how he might really feel when that sandy floor gave way; when his eyes would drink from the vast blue cup that the earth held to his lips.

Uriah is not my son, but he's come closer to being that than anyone else ever will. When Teresa and I fell in love over five years ago, I found myself plunged into the imposing currents of shared motherhood. I proved to be a fearfully resistant swimmer. With the weight of a four-year-old clutching at the loose sleeves of my time, I struggled with the loss of buoyancy. For years, it seemed, I gasped indignantly with the premonition of drowning.

We had become close, nevertheless, in spite of my floundering. Children have a way of etching themselves into the hardest of surfaces. When I looked at the stone upon which I stood, I now saw that amidst the spray-painted, spontaneous graffiti of my life, his name was also written. Just that past autumn we had found a common interest; it was one that amazed us both.

Chasing a long-held desire in the improbable environment of a desert town, I had signed up for classes in scuba diving. Though tactful friends suggested more accessible sports, there was one guy, Uriah, who understood, without question, my determination. After dinner, on the couch, we would marvel together at the underwater photos in my diving magazines. When I finally completed my course, making my open water dives off the shores of Key West, it was Uriah whom I called first with the news of my success. Standing at the pay phone, hair still dripping, engulfed in my wet suit, which felt strikingly similar to being robed in a giant sponge, his voice on the other end of the phone line was ample reward. More gratifying, even, than the newly laminated certification card awaiting me on the counter.

"Really, you did it? You graduated? You're a real scuba diver now? Wow, that's cool!" An hour later, hefting my sodden equipment, I also carried a "Let's Dive" t-shirt, size small, and the matching cap from the dive shop. It rode, even now, upon his head.

It was the dream of learning to dive that made him finally consent to swimming lessons. Teresa and I had encouraged him to take them for years. Though careful never to pressure him with unnecessary demands, his natural love of the water was becoming hindered by the fear of instruction. That winter, sitting on the white resin chair, slippery with chlorinated water, I would seek out the blonde head bobbing in the farthest lane as his teacher yelled out encouragement. On the eve of his final class, I bought him fins. We also promised that one day, late in the school year, we would take him to the sea.

Now, as the three of us slipped off shoes and laid out towels, I hoped that those lessons were enough. Not possessing mask, snorkel, and fins, Teresa would wait for us on the sand. I would take him out for his first swim, alone. His eyes widened as he tested the water. "It's so warm," he said, looking up at me with surprise. "That's right, just like I told you, pal," I answered, handing him the bottle of liquid that we sprayed on our masks to keep them clear. As we rinsed our lenses in the salt water, I wished that clearing my internal view also had such a simple, sudsy solution.

I did not expect him to falter, yet I realized that I must be prepared for it. Even as a confident swimmer, many years before, I had felt the rush of vertigo when, I first donned a mask in the ocean. I remembered well that moment when the floor dropped away, leaving me in unexpected flight a hundred feet above. I knew I could save him if he panicked out there. Yet if he fought me, it would demand my full strength.

I prayed for that assurance that I supposed real mothers felt. Possessing the power of giants as they lifted the car that trapped their child underneath; the psychic instinct that sent them running to the street just before a small foot stepped from the curb. I could never truly attain that ferociously primal wisdom with which mothers of all species protect their young. By his side, instead, was just a slightly sunburned woman who helped him buckle his fin straps. A woman almost shocked to find how much she loved him.

We glided out into the water as gulls soared above us. Stalks of fluted coral brushed our knees. The sun played the only melody in that silent world. It lit the bright bodies of fish as they darted, iridescent, in the gardens of sea plants swayed by tide. For a while we sailed over the shallows in this way, pausing for the tail of a lobster peeking under a rock, the black spines of a sea urchin bristling in a miniature cavern. Yet soon our wanderings led us farther out; I turned my head to see him just as the shelf of land disappeared. Below us, a universe, deeper than midnight. It rolled, whispered, beckoned. Without hesitation, he spread his arms to fly, as at ease as the clouds above us.

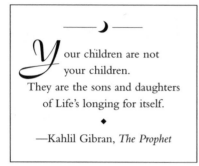

*Y*our children are not your children.
They are the sons and daughters of Life's longing for itself.

◆

—Kahlil Gibran, *The Prophet*

As the round body of a parrot fish appeared far below, he tapped my shoulder and pointed. His face was exuberant in the circle of glass; blue with water light, his eyes were smiling. We followed that gleaming fish for nearly an hour, stopping only to wave to the figure watching from the shore, his mother.

"Maybe one day when he's older we'll dive here together," I thought, even as I reminded myself that adolescence would warrant less cumbersome companions, command different voyages that his heart would follow. Yet as we swam back in the gentle tug of tide, I felt the gift of a truth, a lesson: though what flowed between us was not the voice of blood, it was the quick, blue pulse of water.

Denise M. Spranger juggles writing, painting, and scuba diving along with her "real job" at The Historic Taos Inn in New Mexico. She also strives to be a good co-parent for her partner's son, nurturing in him his desire for oceans on the high desert and whatever dreams, however illogical, he may hold.

✴

About a thousand whales, mostly cows and calves, spend the winter in Baja's Magdalena Bay. We could usually see several in a glance across the water. The Mexican captain of the *Don José*, a double for Anthony Quinn, was very good at approaching pods of whales without frightening them. On the top deck we stood in forests of tripods, long lenses and binoculars, looking down at the enormous bodies beneath the waves, bristly with hitchhiking barnacles and lice.

Calves never left the warmth of their mothers; the pairs moved through the water like roller coasters with sidecars, and there was constant tender touching between them. Often when we approached, the cows would roll over their young calves and play peek-a-boo with us over the broad knobby wall of their mothers' backs.

—Lynn Ferrin, "Big Mothers," *Motorland*

⋆ ⋆ ⋆

Ten Blocks

What makes a walk to school
in the Manhattan rain magical?

I LOVE TRAVELING WITH MY DAUGHTER. AT NEIGHBORHOOD playgrounds she watches, watches. She will carefully climb up the ladder of the slide and climb back down again, cautious, slow. Who, then, is this daredevil who, when traveling, practically runs up mountains? Who delights in clambering over slippery riverbed rocks, finding and losing and finding her balance? I marveled once at the image of her tiny body astride the bare back of a Belgian workhorse. When I went to mount behind her, she firmly declined, then added gently, "Don't worry, Mama." But the distance we travel most together is the ten city blocks between our home and Emma's preschool. In this well-traveled place, my daughter is my teacher.

It's a school morning, grey and drizzly, and we have all overslept. Nevertheless, I'm trying to keep things moving along. Perhaps I'll still be able to get my daughter to school in time for "circle time," her favorite part of the day.

Emma is newly four. Developmentally speaking, four equals oppositional. That's how she figures out that she's not her parents but a separate, unique individual. That's her job. My job, as I see it at the moment, is to accomplish certain tasks of living in spite of this.

I go to brush Emma's hair as she's eating breakfast. She jumps up and runs out of the room as I call after her disappearing form: "Please do *not* run away." The door slams. I don't have time for this. I'm pissed. I find her on my bed, snatch her up, and carry her the length of the apartment back to the breakfast table where her small but clear voice says: "Don't set me down with a bump."

It registers. She's afraid of my anger—which immediately softens. We negotiate the brushing of the hair. She is a force to be reckoned with. Frustration moves in—why does everything have to be negotiated? Just once can't we just get something done efficiently? She's a kid; it shouldn't be this complicated. Besides, she's the one who'll be disappointed to miss circle time. In the end she's distracted and not eating breakfast. When I remind her we need to hurry a bit she says: "Can we have one more slow day before we go back to fast days?"

My heart breaks. This is what the resistance is about—not what happens, but how it happens. Slowly, without agendas. It's understandable considering this is only her second day back at school after a bout of pneumonia. The transition is too abrupt. I realize how unavailable I have been, my thoughts preoccupied with concern over Emma's physical health.

"We can have as many slow days as you want..."

"I want five." She holds up fingers.

"...but the slower you go the more important it is to be mindful and direct when something needs to get done."

"But my mind is jumping around like a monkey—it's here now. Oh, now it's here..." She points to different parts of her head.

"When your mind jumps away, you can bring it back by saying—where am I?"

She is surprised. "At the table."

"What am I doing?"

"Eating breakfast."

"How do I do it? (puzzled look)

She looks puzzled. "Pick up the spoon."

Laughter. Takes a bite.

It becomes a game and we make it through breakfast this way—

where am I? what am I doing? how do I do it? Meanwhile, it's now pouring rain outside. I'm thinking I can make up some time by getting a cab to school this morning instead of walking. Obviously I'm desperate. Emma soon makes it clear she doesn't want to take a cab. Quick, choose, is this a battle worth fighting? Naw, I really don't want to either. It's not so bad out, really, just very wet.

Out on the sidewalk I find that I can't hold an umbrella and push a stroller at the same time. I think of insisting that Emma sit in the stroller and that we "run between the raindrops" to school but something stops me. I turn and look back. Emma is smiling as she walks: big confident strides, umbrella cocked back, rain boots squishing.

Then I realize what she's doing: where am I?—on the sidewalk; what am I doing?—walking in the rain; how do I do it?—put one foot in front of the other. Or some version of that.

At any rate she is fully in the moment, in her environment, and thoroughly enjoying it.

The sensation of the umbrella bumping against a railing brings delighted laughter. Each puddle is a pond, or a rushing stream, depending on its nature. She's absorbed in the details. We find a "pirate key" in the mud at the base of an old gnarled tree and, up the street, a tiny sign precariously perched on the edge of a gutter that says "squirrel." Obviously a clue. We need only find squirrel island on a map to know where to look for the pirate's treasure. A sanitation truck rumbles by. I join Emma in waving to the driver who, impishly, smiles back as he flips us the finger.

Ah, New York. Emma, of course, has no idea the meaning of this particular gesture. She's moved on and is now making "a present" out of things she has found: a few buds freed by last night's storm, bits of colorful plastic, a bottle cap, and a crack vial, together with a mound of mud.

The care she's taking with her arrangement suddenly reminds me of a similar activity in Bali. The Balinese make little offerings that they place outside of their homes and at crossroads two times during the day to appease the evil spirits. These offerings are tiny banana leaf constructions filled with flowers, fruit, rice, and incense. Each one is a miracle of color and placement. As the hours go by, the offerings are squashed by feet and motorcycles, poked at by dogs and chickens, hopefully satiating the evil spirits. While traveling there, I remember loving the idea that, at least once a day, you devote your energy to making something beautiful, making something calm and spellbinding enough to quell the stirrings of the most unsettled spirits. This way even if bad things do happen, you are secure in knowing that you have done your best to calm the storm. As if aware of my thoughts, Emma looks up from her creation: "When people die they become the moons over different countries, but their spirits stay here and they like to see pretty things."

The stroller's too bulky to fold up and carry, so by the time we reach school a sizable puddle has formed in the seat and I'm drenched. Emma's wet in front from the sling-back approach to carrying her umbrella. But for the last three or four blocks she's been singing...

> Drip drip drop
> little April showers
> what can compare with your beautiful sound
> beautiful sound
> beautiful sound?

We missed circle time. But, of course, we almost missed a lot more. The teacher greets us and says, "She looks really good today, really healthy."

She is. She is.

Terry Strother lives with her small family in New York City. She struggles to balance a life of adventure and motherhood while teaching yoga part-time and continuing her efforts to write and travel. Her writing has appeared in Travelers' Tales: A Woman's World *and she was the winner of Travelers'*

Tales's first writing contest. Emma Strother dreams of living in a warm place where she can "have bare legs all the time and feel things with my feet."

★

Do you remember
when you were a baby
and looked up at the sky
and wiggled and waggled?
I could sing to you 'til the fire flies.

and she folded up her hands to see the
black night.
"It's all right," her mother said
and nudged her.

—Emma Strother, age 4

PAMELA MICHAEL

* * *

Over the River and Through the Woods

A family searches for home ground and each other.

I HADN'T MEANT TO KILL MY GRANDMOTHER, OF COURSE, ONLY
to surprise her. But the shock of my unexpected appearance—all
the way from California—right on the front steps of St. Joseph's
Nursing Home was apparently too much for her: she clutched her
chest, stumbled, then fell onto my father's shepherding arm. A
small "ohhhh" floated out of her mouth like a vapor. I froze in horror, giddy grin melting down my chin.

Nanacide.

Would I ever be able to forgive myself?

Forgiveness, for this act at least, was unnecessary. Nana was startled and shaken but alive. My impromptu family reunion was off
to a rocky start.

The plan had seemed so clever three days earlier when I
boarded a Greyhound bus on a lark, spurred on by my husband,
who had seized on an offhand wish that I could rendezvous with
my parents and sister, who were driving from the East Coast to
visit my father's mother, a grandmother I adored, but hadn't seen
in years.

"Go! You should go! Surprise them all—wouldn't it be fun? Just show up," he said, then continued gently, with a squeeze of my shoulder. "It's summer. Take a little vacation. You deserve it."

I didn't know until the divorce six years later, of course, that my husband's enthusiasm for my trip was fueled by the fact that it would be much easier for him to fool around behind my back if my back were in LaCrosse, Wisconsin.

At the time, though, I was touched by his concern and didn't need much convincing; Nana *was* old and I *did* need a break. The prospect of a solo adventure was compelling to a woman who'd been a mother since nineteen and had traveled little. I embraced the idea with gusto and quickly concocted a playful scheme to make the trip all the more fun: I would arrive before my parents, have a joyful reunion with my grandmother, then wheel her into the lounge or TV room or whatever common space St. Joseph's might have, don a red hooded-sweatshirt purchased just for the occasion, get into her bed and pop up from under the covers when my parents entered her room—a mirthful, twisted send up of *Little Red Riding Hood* that twenty years later I can't imagine dreaming up, much less following through on.

But there I was the very next day, burrowed in at the back of the bus, where, as in high school, the "bad boys" still congregated. Cowboys and Indians, gamblers, vagabonds, runaways, drunks, and me—all headed east in a miasma of diesel fumes, cigarette smoke, sweat, and urine stench from the tiny on-board lavatory nearby. I was relegated to the rear Smoking Section because I then had a three-pack-a-day nicotine habit. No matter how many cigarettes I smoked on that trip, however, I could barely sit still. I bristled with excitement and anticipation of the surprise. I chuckled to myself across eight states, imagining the looks on everyone's faces, the laughs we would have, the sweetness of at least part of our scattered family together once again in the place where my grandparents grew up, a "home ground," if we had such a thing.

We were a mobile bunch, Irish and Norwegian immigrants on my father's side, who settled for a while in the rich Wisconsin farmland; but like so many Americans, and Midwesterners in particular, it seems, were ever ready to set out for new landscapes and horizons. It was as if once a family emigrated, wrenched them- selves away from their roots and kin for whatever good reason, they had trouble knowing when or where to stop, or where they belonged. By the end of World War II, we were strewn across the American landscape like shrapnel, fragments of a living type of kinship that existed only in brief phone calls, birthday cards, and occasional holiday visits.

My father's parents left Wisconsin for Wyoming shortly after their wedding and later settled outside of Chicago. My own par- ents couldn't wait to get out of the Midwest when I was a child. They finally made the break when I was six, moving up and down the eastern seaboard more than a dozen times before I left home at eighteen. They regarded the friends they left behind in the lovely tree-shaded Illinois town where they were raised as provin- cial and unadventurous. Many undoubtedly were, but as a child being dragged from school to school and neighborhood to neigh- borhood, I longed to live in just such a place, surrounded by those I had known for years.

Indeed, it came as quite a surprise to find myself with a grow- ing sense of warmth and security as I traveled toward the Midwest, headed "home" on the bus. Perhaps I was a child of the prairie after all.

Once out of California, the bus hurled through the stark loamy rangelands of Nevada, where we lost most of the gamblers. We lumbered into Utah and Salt Lake City at 3 a.m., a surreal sight made more otherworldly by the theatrically-lit Mormon Temple, and continued across the Great Divide into Wyoming and Casper, where my father was born in 1921. My grandfather, who had a law degree from the University of Wisconsin, had moved the family to Wyoming and gone to work for the Chicago, Burlington & Quincy Railroad, rather than practice. The railroad company trained him how to crack open safes found in many of the aban- doned towns they were buying up throughout the West, to make sure there were no deeds or documents that could cloud their title or right-of-way. Casper, glimpsed fleetingly from the ride into the downtown bus station (no city's most scenic route) was wind-whipped and desolate. I couldn't help thinking to myself: if it still looked like the Wild West in 1977, what a place it must have been in 1921.

After Wyoming came the Nebraska prairies, then Iowa (home to many of my mother's ancestors), Minnesota, and finally Wisconsin and the Mississippi River, gouged out of the land by the mammoth glaciers of the Great Ice Age. The entire trip had seemed like riding across the surface of a map, as if the half continent I had just crossed had been reduced to the few landmarks customarily noted on a road map: highways, towns, state lines, rivers, mountains. From the moving window the road was all, the terrain merely something you moved *through,* devoid of the details that define "place"—people, stories, animals, history, time.

My timing, or rather Greyhound's, was just a little off: my parents and sister had arrived ahead of me and were on their way out to lunch with Nana in tow when my taxi pulled up in front. "There goes the Red Riding Hood prank," I thought, "but at least I'll be able to make a dramatic entrance."

They all saw me at once, or so it seemed, toppling into each other as if a shock wave had hit them, their eyes wide, confused, and disbelieving, frightened even. This was not the way I had envisioned the big moment at all.

When my grandmother faltered, I was certain I had killed her. In an instant, the barely-containable delight I had sustained for two and a half days, over two thousand miles, changed to panic. It felt as if I had entered a nightmare from which I might not awaken. My guilt and horror, however, were (blessedly) short-lived: I had forgotten Nana's years of theatrical training at the Celtic Academy of Hypochondria and her flair for high medical drama; she had never been one to say "ouch" when a shriek or swoon would do. (Though some would say that a woman who bled for 28 days out of every 30 for her entire fertile life, as she had, was entitled to every ounce of sympathy, manipulated or not, that she could muster.) Her heart, however theatrically clutched, was strong enough to withstand the shock of seeing me; it was strong enough to sustain her another five years, in fact. Dying that day—in the arms of her son, surrounded by family—might have been a kinder fate, though; instead she spent the next five years bedridden, visited only occasionally by distant, dutiful relations, the grown children of second cousins and such, her immediate family too impoverished, crazed, or aloof to get themselves to Wisconsin to see her. She died alone at the age of 92.

I had been her first and favorite grandchild, the daughter she never had. Her home had been a haven for me as a child, a place of rich dark mahogany window sills, glistening chandeliers, large comfy furniture, and heavy drapes that blocked out harsh sun and loud noises. I remember it as cool inside and smelling of lemon oil, moth balls, pipe tobacco, and burnt sugar, which somehow combined into a delicious mix. I spent as much time there as I could and often had to be carried back home crying after a weekend or overnight visit.

I loved the order and predictability of my grandparent's home, knowing that breakfast every morning would be oatmeal with the cream from the top of the milk bottle, saved just for me; that being in the kitchen meant wearing an apron and that going to the store meant wearing a hat; that there was always a note pad holder with a silver pen attached to it by a chain next to the telephone, which sat on a narrow table in its own little telephone table alcove off the living room; that Monday was laundry day when we'd go to the basement and feed wet clothes through wooden rollers to wring them out before hanging them outside on the metal clotheslines that Nana had first wiped clean with a rag. I loved that my grandfather came home at the same time every evening and sat in the same chair and puffed on his pipe while asking me about my day. I loved knowing which scented drawer held the terrible/wonderful neckpiece of flattened foxes that bit each other's tails with braided silk-covered lower jaws and which held the threadbare padded-velvet photo album I poured over obsessively, asking again and again about the old-fashioned people peering out from tintypes and faded photos and about how they were related to me.

My favorite picture was of my grandparents and some friends, all probably in their early twenties, standing six abreast across the wooden roadway of a small one-lane iron bridge. My grandmother and another woman wear long linen skirts and cotton blouses tucked into tiny waistbands, brooches at their necks; the men are in baggy suits. They are all wearing hats—big straw sunhats for the women, and bowlers and straw boaters for the men, some tilted rakishly, others set comically on back on the head, or over one eye. The friends stand, each in an engaging and different pose, with arms linked or thrown over each other's shoulders, beaming at the camera. Looking at this photo in recent years (it's one of the few scraps of family history to have survived my family's nomadism), I am struck by the easy camaraderie of these young adults—the uncomplicated good cheer and most of all, the innocence in their expressions, particularly my grandparents.

And yet their lives can't have been easy. Their's was a "mixed" marriage. My grandmother was Irish Catholic and my grandfather the son of a stern Norwegian Lutheran immigrant. My grandfather never converted, exactly, but he attended Mass with my grandmother every week, contributed to church renovation funds and mission appeals, and eventually became an officer in their parish. Even this lifetime of devotion (to my grandmother, if not the Church) was not enough to get him into a Catholic cemetery when he died. It broke my grandmother's heart. True believer that she was, she despaired of reuniting with him in heaven because he hadn't been buried in consecrated ground.

Both Nana and Gaca, as I called my grandfather, came from families of thirteen children. My grandmother's father, Michael Kelly, drank himself to death in his 40s, when she was four or five. Her mother managed to keep the family together by cleaning houses the rest of her life.

My grandfather survived Wisconsin winters in a log cabin and had been kicked in the head by a mule while sitting in his father's lap in the front of a buckboard at the age of three. He had a metal plate in his forehead as a consequence, with a horseshoe-shaped dent that always fascinated me as a child. He almost didn't survive the diabetes, though, that struck him down as a young father. He was on his death bed when insulin was newly formulated for human use, and was one of the first people ever to receive it.

My father's older brother (and years later, my own son) ultimately developed diabetes as well. My grandmother's entire life became devoted to monitoring food intake, exercise levels, bowel movements, and sleep patterns of two family members, leaving my father feeling a bit ignored, he always said. The strict regimen required by diabetics, as well as my grandmother's unending menstruation, took a toll. That burden, plus a kind of Irish *oh-go-on-with-ye-now-I-don't-have-time-for-your-shenanigans* brusqueness, combined to make my grandmother a rather stern killjoy, of sorts. She was, no doubt, a difficult mother, especially for my irrepressible father, who, unable to divert his mother's attention from the somewhat obsessive care of his father and brother, became a child radio star at nine.

> The surname Kelly derives from the *kelles*, priestesses of an Irish prehistoric hierophantic clan, devoted to the Goddess Kele, a cognate of the Saxon word Kale, or Mother Earth. Kale, along with other similarly named deities in Asia, Europe, and the Middle East, trace their roots back to Kali, the Hindu Goddess of creation, preservation, and destruction, the archetypal image of birth and death mother.
>
> ◆
>
> —MB & PM

But grandparenting is the ultimate second chance and Nana became an attentive, funny, and nurturing grandmother, particularly with me. I intuitively saw through her brusqueness as a child and played to it, melting her resistance. She was quick to snipe, to be sure, but for me, just as quick to hug and always ready to tickle my back—"Oh, just a few more minutes, Nana, please." With the self-centeredness of a child, I loved her probably more for how much she loved me than for who she was. But I loved her with a passion.

Her quick Irish tongue didn't frighten me a bit; on the contrary, I was charmed by it and mimicked it and fed it back to her with a twinkle in my eye. I loved the music of her language, with its magical Irish words like *shilalegh, leprechaun, blarney,* and *wee.*

Nana's jokes were often self-deprecating and her delivery was deadpan and deadly. I remember her whispering to me one Sunday in church as her friend Mrs. O'Malley walked up the aisle to communion, "You know, God loved Irish women so much he gave them permission to wear their legs upside down."

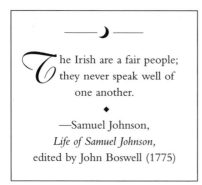

The Irish are a fair people; they never speak well of one another.

♦

—Samuel Johnson,
Life of Samuel Johnson,
edited by John Boswell (1775)

So, there we were, together again, crying and laughing and exclaiming on the steps of St. Joseph's.

"You little dickens, Pammie! How did you get here?"

"By bus, Nana. I took the bus."

"Saints preserve us! With Lord knows what kind of riffraff."

"It was fun. I wanted to surprise you."

"Kill me is more like it. You devil, you."

The sharp tongue hadn't dulled in the years since I'd seen her; that helped me to deal with the reality of her unsteady gait and frailty. My parents had aged, too. The sister I hardly knew, just five when I left home, had become a sweet but frighteningly servile young woman of eighteen. We were five strangers, really, straining to conjure up memories and shared histories, separated by distance and finances and the distractions of urban living, like so many postwar American families.

"Why don't you take us on a tour of LaCrosse, Nana?" I suggested. "Dad's got a car; you can tell him where to drive or we can get a map. We can visit the house where you grew up and your old school, and Doerflinger's Department Store where you worked, and Granddad's Bluff where your cousin fell off the cliff and died."

"Reaching over the rail to pick flowers for his mother on Mother's Day," my grandmother added, recounting one of the more memorable cautionary tales of my childhood. "But why would I want to see those places again?" she continued, contrary as usual. "It was so long ago. Everything's changed, anyway. Everyone's gone. Like Dad."

My grandmother had made mourning her husband's death some twenty years earlier a part of her persona—it was not what she did, it was who she was. No joyous occasion, no birthday or graduation or holiday, could ever be celebrated without her breaking down into sobs about his absence and fleeing the table, church, party—wherever we happened to be—in grief, then going into a deep depression for days.

We had witnessed many of these sad, but after-a-point tedious displays over the years; she visited us quite regularly after Gaca's death at sixty-eight, eventually becoming a member of the airlines' Million Mile Club, unfortunately in the days before frequent flyer benefits. Her casual and willing attitude toward travel, out of character in so many ways with the cautious person she was, gave me a new appreciation of her when I was a child, and her example and pluck were important to me as a woman traveler later in life. But as her health and my parents' personal lives deteriorated, the visits became fewer and fewer. There were times when she didn't know where they were, when I didn't know where they were, when we were lost to each other.

My parents' fortunes had always been up and down. For the moment at least, those fortunes were ascending. Now, here they were, taking a summer vacation from their long winter of bankruptcy and other horrors; we were all eager to recapture the somewhat romanticized glory of seasons past. We cajoled and wheedled Nana into saying yes and set off in a Buick in search of our history, or at least a decent lunch.

Pamela Michael is a freelance writer and radio producer. She is the co-founder and director of The River of Words Project, an international children's environmental poetry and art contest, sponsored by International Rivers Network and The Library of Congress. She lives in Berkeley, California with a Tibetan Terrier named Yeti, who—aside from several abominable personal habits—is the perfect menopausal companion.

★

It's sunset in late Fall. I am with my mom and dad in their board-and-care home, watching the sky turn dark pink. The leafless branches of the tall, sprawling trees through the window look like elegant black lace against the sky. My dad is slumped in his wheelchair, asleep, the devastation of Alzheimer's disease having taken its toll. But he still understands the meaning of my hug, a kiss, or my caring hands clasping his. My mom forgets her pain momentarily as we talk about the beauty of those trees, which reflect every change of season. Another day ends. A new year begins. The renewal of life continues.

—Suzie Coxhead, "Images"

GABRIELLA DE FERRARI

*   *   *

Mother's Cooking

Sustenance for the heart comes
from a Peruvian kitchen.

OUR KITCHEN WAS A LARGE ROOM COVERED WITH WHITE AND
blue tiles. It had generous windows that opened onto the garden,
ample counters, and a large table in the middle, where the maids
congregated for their meals and, during their free hours, listened
to the radio-novelas. The kitchen was a laboratory in constant
operation, where everyone worked to produce Mother's experiments. Mother's cooking was a reflection of her approach to
life, filled with enthusiasm and desire for the new. I often think
that it must have been born of the monotony of her early life in
the convent.

Even simple breakfasts of hot chocolate and toast were the
products of elaborate preparation. The jams were made at home
from fruit so ripe no sugar was used. There were many varieties:
mulberry, apricot, tangerine, and Mother's specialty, tomato jam,
made with bitter almonds with an unusual, piquant flavor.
Mother's cuisine combined the cooking of her native Italy, learned
from the nuns, the cooking of Peru, and French recipes from her
magazines. It was a fragrant and delicate cuisine, in which no flavor or ingredient dominated but they all blended in pleasing, unexpected harmony.

117

Food arrived at the table as a small triumph that Mother loved to share with her family, especially with Father, who was an abstemious but sophisticated eater. To the corn dishes she learned to prepare in Peru, she added her own touches, such as a bit of saffron and some pine nuts. Her pastas, which as a child I loved to see roll out of the cutter, were a specialty all her own. Sometimes they were filled with porcini mushrooms from Italy, fava beans mashed with sweet potatoes and onions, or eggplant and fresh oregano. At other times they were served with one of an endless variety of sauces, made with zucchini flowers, sea urchins, veal marrow, baby avocados, or walnuts—some heavy and wintery, some light and spirited, depending on the season and the ripeness of the vegetables. Even the simple tomato-and-basil sauce was special. It was only made on those few days of summer when the tomatoes were perfectly ripe.

In the summer we ate grilled fish and octopus with tender salads and stuffed vegetables. When it got cool, a rarity in the desert, Mother, nostalgic for Italy, would serve pork roasts surrounded by potatoes in a spicy pepper sauce. For Easter we had baked stuffed baby goat, succulent with the scent of rosemary, accompanied by artichokes and peas. The Christmas turkey arrived at the table stuffed with chestnuts, wild rice, and sage, surrounded by asparagus. Desserts were the culmination of every meal. I can still see the mountains of tiny puff pastries stuffed with a cherimoya cream and held together by caramel, the Napoleon cake layered with guava sauce, crunchy and light, and the homemade ice creams rich with chunks of pomegranates and peaches.

The ingredients that arrived at Mother's kitchen were the result of an elaborate gathering process. A great majority came from our own garden; the rest Mother found in the marketplace, where she became an expert on foods both local and imported. There, like the rest of the women of my town, she became a huntress in pursuit of perfection. Mother knew how to tell the ripeness of a pineapple by the texture of its skin, the freshness of a fish by the amount of moisture in its eyes, and the hotness of a pepper by the shade of its skin.

Twice a week, early in the morning, she went to the market. I loved going with her and watching her move among the piles of fresh fruits and vegetables. Fruits included papayas and guavas from the jungle, apples and peaches from Chile, sweet juicy grapes, oranges, and pomegranates from the local farms—products of the desert that never knew morning dew and were ripened only by the caress of the sun. The vegetable counters were equally plentiful. Mother learned to distinguish among the thirty-odd varieties of potatoes available. Purple ones were to be used with cheese sauces, porous yellow ones for stews, firm white ones for frying. She pinched, sniffed, and weighed the vegetables until she found the right ones. As a child I tried hard to learn these skills, but when my turn came to use them as a young bride in America, they were useless to me. I discovered that tomatoes came in plastic boxes, apples were sealed in plastic bags, and corn was only sold frozen.

Mother was at her best on Fridays, when the fishermen's wives took over the market. They brought with them the bounties of the Pacific: tiny fish such as anchovies and sardines, huge slabs of swordfish and bonito, and the fruits of the sea, urchins, clams, crabs, and lobsters. Because we had a refrigerator at home and could store a large amount of fish, Mother was a favored customer. The fishwives saved her corbina to make *ceviche,* the Peruvian kind, with lime juice and olive oil, and clams of all sizes and colors for her risottos.

Mother was good at bargaining. She would struggle to find something wrong with a vegetable in order to get a good price, or she would tactfully point out that someone else was selling the same merchandise for less. All the women of my town bargained. It was a chance for the housewives to display a skill, to feel the power of their knowledge.

The market was also where housewives exchanged gossip and recipes. I still smile to myself when I remember the day Mother overheard two housewives talking about an unusual way to prepare a turkey for a gourmet death. She rushed home to persuade Father and Pablo, our gardener, to try out the new method. For a week the two men force-fed a turkey five spoonfuls of brandy a day followed by a handful of nuts. Every time I eat turkey, I remember Mother's bird wobbling happily in a drunken stupor. When we finally ate it, it had a wonderful flavor that I have never encountered since.

When the marketing was done, two hours after Mother began, she filled the car with baskets and we headed for home. As soon as we got there, it was time to start the interminable process of scrubbing and drying the food. Later everything would be wrapped in white paper, labeled, and stored.

Mother was like a dancer in the kitchen. She appeared about an hour before mealtime, after everything was already washed and chopped. Everyone was on alert, waiting for the magician who would mix and stir everything together to create a tour de force. She moved swiftly and intuitively, led by her internal music. Sometimes she followed a recipe carefully, concentrating intently. Then everyone knew to be very quiet. She never tasted anything, but seemed to make decisions based on the color and fragrance of the food. When everything was done, she would ring the old church bell on the patio to announce that the meal would be served. Radiantly, she would wait for her family, beaming with the pleasure of having put together a good meal.

Meals were served in our dining room, which overlooked the green lawn bordered with flowers. It was a room suffused in light. The tablecloths were beautifully pressed, the silver and china re-

> "*M*ama treats food the way dancers treat empty space..." read the inscription on a signed photo of Rudolf Nureyev on the wall of Mama's, a shack restaurant in Panahachel, Guatemala (Lake Atitlan) in the 1970s. You had to ford a river to get there, but it was well worth the trek—fresh fish, vegetables grown in her own garden, platters of cornbread, and big pitchers of lemonade on every table.
>
> ◆
>
> —MB & PM

splendent. At the center of the table, a large bowl of flowers, usually sweet peas or roses, gently caught the tones of the tablecloth. From the windows we could see the hummingbirds having their own feast in the hibiscus flowers, and we would hear canaries on the patio in the distance.

After lunch we took long walks in the garden, accompanied by our guardian Doberman dogs. Soon Pablo would arrive through the large colonial gate. As Mother's dedicated partner, he never questioned her agricultural experiments. When Mother returned from her trips abroad, she brought seeds and cuttings, which Pablo patiently nourished into bloom. Every time a new flower grew, it was cause for celebration. When the first nasturtium opened or the first raspberry ripened, Pablo would just shake his head and murmur, "A miracle."

He and mother made an unusual pair. Mother moved with the speed of light; Pablo moved slowly, as if in a perpetual state of tiredness. He was the only person I ever knew who could sleep standing up. When we were young, we loved to wake him up. Yet Pablo is still there. Now almost eighty-five years old, he has worked for my family for more than fifty years and knows the history of every plant and every tree in the garden.

When I saw him last year, it broke my heart to hear him apologize for the garden's looking so overgrown. Together we cut white roses—Mother's favorites, the most beautiful and fragrant of all roses—to take to my parents' grave.

Gabriella De Ferrari is an art historian and the author of the critically acclaimed novel, A Cloud on the Sand, *and a memoir,* Gringa Latina, *from which this story was excerpted. She is a contributing editor of* Travel and Leisure *and* House and Garden, *and lives in New York City and Connecticut.*

✳

Space filled with the presence of mothers, and the place where everyone is a daughter. *Space which doesn't exist without matter.* The place where she predominates. *Space which is never separate from matter.* The space shaped by the movements of white-haired women and ringing with the laughter of old lady friends. The world seen on the faces of middle-aged women. The place filled with the love of women for women. Space shaped by the play of the littlest girls.

The stone dropped in water. Space that knows her. *Starlight in darkness.* Space lit up with her thoughts. *The circle in space.* Space dancing under her broom. Space transformed in her kitchen.

—Susan Griffin, *Woman and Nature: The Roaring Inside Her*

JOYCE WILSON

* * *

Christmas in Cairo

*A mother and daughter get more
than they bargained for.*

WE PASSED THROUGH THE GLASS DOORS BENEATH THE RED EXIT
sign and stood on the brink of the city in the pea-green darkness.
I hailed a bearded man in a dark suit—"Taxi! Taxi?"—only to
watch him shrug and wander away. My mother and I were often
thrown together like this, I thought, abandoned against the elements. Since my father's death, I had found myself on my own
with my mother repeatedly, even though by now she had remar-
ried, and I was married with a daughter.

The initiative for this trip to Egypt had come from her. She
proposed combining work (at a conference on the environment)
with pleasure (sightseeing on the Nile), and she invited me to join
her. Our underlying agenda was a special journey in memory of
the deceased: my father had often claimed that Cairo had been his
favorite city.

Soon three men approached us from out of nowhere. The first
introduced himself as a driver. I looked over his shoulder at the
bearded man who had ignored us before; now he was smiling and
nodding. Ah, I thought, he understood after all. The taxi driver
handed our baggage over to the two long-robed men, and my
heart sank as I watched them heave all our belongings into the

123

trunk of the cab. Thousands of miles from home, I mused, and at the mercy of the male preconception that women need an entourage of assistants.

The taxi carried us through the streets of the city under the cover of thick velvet darkness. I grasped the belly of my handbag and breathed a sigh of relief once I felt the hard edge of my book inside. I had imagined it on the plane, left behind and forgotten. The volume of Egyptian folklore described the darkness as the arched body of the goddess Nut, her feet at one edge of the horizon and her hands at the other, who bent over the land and swallowed the sun every evening, causing night, only to give birth to it again every morning, creating day. I was not consoled by the continuity of this myth. The reference to pregnancy was enough to awaken pangs of anxiety in my mind, where birth, separation, and death were all wrenching passages to recall from beginning to end, leaving the individual battered and spent at every step of the way.

Traveling with my mother in a foreign country, I sometimes felt like a climber clinging white-knuckled to the side of a cliff. It seemed that old distances were widening between us, requiring new ground rules to maintain comfortable intimacies. In the back of the taxi, my mother sat upright like a formidable queen. Her white hair and pale features, her skin—seldom tanned in her later years—glowed with a luminous beauty. She was clearly in command of her own life. Her gray eyes beneath pale lashes were fixed on the next frontier. She would ride with composure to the gallows, I thought wryly.

"Who was Semiramis?" Mother asked the cab driver. He turned and regarded us.

"A goddess," he said simply. Later he broke the silence to announce, "There is the local mosque." We turned our heads and strained our necks to see the place of worship, visible through the window for a matter of seconds as we flew through the city.

Climbing out of the taxi at the Semiramis Intercontinental Hotel, we argued about who would give how much to tip the driver before we pushed our luggage through the revolving doors to the inside. I couldn't help but notice that my mother was the vision of health. Attractive and capable and headstrong as ever, she insisted on carrying her own bags, pulling the larger one on its own tiny wheels that tripped and jumped and rocked off balance at every change in the floor's surface. Yet her self-assurance, displayed as she announced our arrival to the impeccably dressed man behind the hotel desk, seemed tinged with an unfamiliar frailty. I saw it in the man's eyes, kind behind his glasses, and I felt it in my own throat.

Once our duties at the conference had ended, my mother and I were free for twenty-four hours to explore the city before joining our party of Americans on the Nile, where an old steamer would take us sightseeing to upper Egypt and back. We set out on our own for the Egyptian Museum right after breakfast. As we walked past the life-sized figure of Santa Claus astride a camel in the hotel lobby and moved beyond range of the Christmas jingles broadcast continually over the intercom, I was plagued with speculations. Aside from her advancing age, my mother's self-confidence caused me to clench my jaw. In this exotic city, my mother was beautiful in an unadorned way. She was a vibrant woman in the prime of life who expressed her delight overtly; yet, in this city of fundamentalists, her manner might be seen as irreverent, even immoral. That was what worried me.

I scanned the face of the *maître d'hôtel* for signs of disapproval.

> ———◗———
>
> *M*others and wives who travel begin to claim rights of financial independence, leadership qualities, assertiveness, confidence, a sense of self, peer esteem, physical stature, strength, sexual impregnability, and creditability. When a woman is empowered with these rights, her societal role is more similarly situated and equal to men. Once she experiences this liberation, travel becomes not just a temporary self liberation, not a necessary personal tonic but an addictive drug for her social equilibrium.
>
> ◆
>
> —Martha Dundon,
> "Women Who Travel"

He warned us about the traffic, summarizing all the accounts we'd heard about the Egyptian style of driving: lots of instinct, no rules, few traffic lights, the exhilaration of manning the steering wheel. At first I found the chaos on the city streets amusing. But after standing on the street corner for minutes while an unmitigated stream of traffic flowed by, I reconsidered my mother's health, her age, and a daughter's duty, and thought that perhaps we should put this excursion off until after lunch.

"Don't cross there," a man warned us. "Follow me. Down this way. Here, let me take your hand."

He was about five-foot-five, with dark brown skin and a physique based on roundness. His head seemed perfectly round, his torso a protruding globe. He was dressed in a light gray wool suit with shoes that resembled flat mules, triangular-toed and backless like slippers, making him scuffle when he walked. His arms moved with a buoyant energy.

I saw with horror that my mother was quite taken with him. She responded amiably while I tagged along behind, sinking into a meditation on suspicion. He said he was from Nubia, in upper Egypt, raised in a family of nine children. But now, married himself, he had only five children. "Five is enough," he said. "Any more is too much. Too expensive." He rubbed his thumb against his fingers. My mother remarked that she had two daughters, one of them at her side.

He exclaimed, "Really? And you are so young! I thought you must be sisters!"

"With my white hair?" Mother laughed. "I'm almost sixty-eight."

"Sixty-eight! No! It could not be true! This one is the youngest? The oldest! You both are so young!" He then offered two camels and four goats for my hand in marriage. "Just joking," he said.

When we told him we were on our way to the museum, he looked at his watch and said, "So early? It does not open until eleven. Don't you know that Tuesdays and Fridays are holy days?

Everything is closed in the early mornings for prayer." I was perplexed and wondered why no one at the hotel had told us of this.

He showed us how to cross through the center of Cairo underground, safely away from cars. As we walked with him, or rather, followed him, he asked us where we were from, what we did. He drew a quick breath at my mother's response. "Institute!" he said. He himself was a manager of a shop owned by his father. They grew flowers, dahlias and lotus, then made scents from them.

As soon as I realized that we were being escorted to his shop, I stopped in my tracks and said we weren't interested. But my mother deferred to him. "These experiences don't come along everyday," she whispered to me over her shoulder. "I think we should follow through." She walked quickly behind the jubilant man. My concerns about my mother were replaced by a new foreboding.

Turning off the main square into a short alley, we entered the shop. The experience had all the magic and charm of passing through a threshold between different worlds. I was sure I could hear tinkling cymbals and feel the lifting of veils as we walked into a room of mirrors and glass shelving, displaying a menagerie of small colorful bottles. Some were like small flasks, with long necks and broad bowls; others were cylindrical and decorated with hand painted flowers and curlicues. We met the father and proprietor of the shop, a man bigger and taller than his son. His hair, kinky and gray, was receding and revealed an oblong callous on his forehead from regular worship at the mosque.

We sat on a broad misshapen sofa and drank small glasses of sugary mint tea. The son set out liter bottles full of yellowish and murky green oil. "These never change color," he said, opening a phial and then spreading the liquid on our wrists with a glass pipette. "This one is from lotus blossoms, this from the jasmine. Here is one called Christmas night," he said smiling to me. "It will make your husband love you!"

Soon he was readying to measure the scents into bottles; I suggested the smallest ones. "How many would you like? Six? This size usually costs twenty pounds," he said. "But I will give you a good price."

I knew my mother seldom wore perfume at all. I offered, "Three for twenty."

His face fell. "You have a good daughter, Madame." He sighed. "For three? But one is worth twenty."

Soon prices were flying back and forth, and we were settling on four kinds of scents, measured into bottles with delicate glass stoppers and wrapped in cotton for the journey home. We also chose six paintings individually designed on genuine papyrus leaves, crushed into a small wad and then released to show their authenticity, and a hematite necklace. I was nearly enjoying a position of privilege, choosing and discarding, except for a sinking feeling at the pit of my stomach. My heart gave when I saw my mother produce her credit card. We spent over two hundred pounds on trifles.

I thought my mother must be losing her mind. She had never approved of acquiring things. Normally she displayed a Quaker's deep-seated resistance to purchasing anything beyond bare necessities. But now in Cairo she was cutting loose. I took another look at her and saw a vivacious woman with a flushed face, exclaiming and laughing, really enjoying herself. I had never known my mother to indulge in such pleasure.

"I have a son in San Francisco," said our Nubian friend, who now guided us to the underground passageway that would lead us to the museum. "When I come to America, I will come to your house, and you can make me a cup of coffee."

We parted in a flurry of smiles and niceties. His parting words of advice: don't buy the papyrus on the streets, don't buy the green bananas, and don't pay for a guide at the museum entrance.

We proceeded to the museum through the clean well-traveled underground thoroughfare. We seemed to be the only women out and about in a city populated by men.

It wasn't long before we discovered that, of course, the museum had been open for hours and it was not yet eleven o'clock. Once inside we were quickly exhausted after a quick solitary run-through of King Tut's tomb and the mummies. Returning to the courtyard, the low angle of the winter sun bore into our eyes, nearly blinding our sight.

On the way back, we did not use the underground. I was sure I could see the hotel above the other buildings and made my way through the parking lot straight for it. Every hawker descended on my mother. Something about her, her looks, her manner, her reluctance to be rude, her eagerness to take up the rope whenever conversation went slack, egged them on. I was shocked to see something I had never detected before in my mother, her eagerness to be liked. I found myself shouting at the Egyptians as I wanted to shout at my mother, "No! No!" A thousand times no. I had become the elder, my mother the younger.

A slim man with a black mustache asked if we were staying at the Hotel Inter-Continental. "I've seen you there," he said. "I work in the arcade. And I'm on my way now. Can I escort you?"

He asked what we had bought. "Scents and papyrus," we told him "How much for the scents?" he asked. "And the papyrus?"

He grew stern and said we had paid much too much. "You can get six of those for ten pounds," he said. And we had spent, how much? One hundred? He said he owned a jewelry shop nearby; would we like to come look at some silver? Our spirits low, we easily dismissed him.

"Taken for a ride!" my mother said as we entered the dim interior of the lobby. "Fed a line. And we fell for it. The museum open at eleven, papyrus for ten pounds a piece, scents for I don't know how much!"

In the hotel room, as I took the perfumes out of the paper wrapping, I felt slightly nauseated. The heavy, cloying smell that once seemed so weighted with exoticism was overwhelming.

"It's the hypocrisy I can't stand," my mother said. "All that baloney about us being sisters. It's such a line. Meaningless."

I consoled her by offering a number of alternative viewpoints, none terribly convincing. We had experienced an initiation into a foreign culture; we made a connection with a man who might contact us once we returned to the States; we had acquired personal objects that might take on more meaning with time. We have to conclude, I said, as Paul Fussell has, that, this being the end of the twentieth century, we are not explorers in an undiscovered land but tourists on a shopping spree.

"It's all meaningless," my mother sighed. Suddenly she stood in front of me and looked into my eyes as through the frame of a glass. "Tell me what you think," she queried me. "About your father. Do you really believe that he is close to us, even after death?"

The question was so direct, it left me speechless. "Well, yes," I said. "Or rather, no. I do feel his presence sometimes, but I don't believe I know where he is. I envision a space...." I was stumbling. "I pray to envision the space where he is very clearly."

"It's garbage," my mother was saying. "He's not anywhere. There is no life after death. I have known that since Sunday school, when I decided never to go back. And I never did."

She was pouting. Nearly seventy, my mother seemed on the verge of puberty. I took a hard look into the future. Eventually, I knew I would have to take charge, but when? I wanted suddenly to secure my mother's protection. Isn't dying like passing into a different culture? You surprise a hunger in yourself. As your ability to reason dissolves, your last thoughts will be, "No, I never suspected that it would be like this. Surely someone should have told me," and you relinquish the familiar for a sudden entry, like a compulsion.

"Still, I believe there is a reincarnation," my mother was saying. "I'm sure we come back as the air we breathe!" She smiled at me like a child.

But I want to be there, I thought with a sudden vehemence. I want to be the one to escort my mother to the other side. No one else will understand her well enough. Understand what? I nearly laughed out loud at my own thoughts. I could see how necessary it would be to plead my mother's special case at the gates after death. Still, I could do it. I have the tenacity and forbearance to see my mother through to the "right place." I can shut my eyes and imagine her into a heaven of cool grasses and quiet plentiful streams.

At the Citadel, we walked through the carpeted theater of the mosque with a female guide, an attractive young woman with long dark hair. I listened to her description of the practice of wearing the veil, the attitudes pro and con, and couldn't stop myself from pursuing the issue. Was the reasoning to hide the lower half of the face or the whole of the hair? How did this guide feel about it? Was it only a religious practice? The more I wanted to know from this woman, the more irritated I could see her become. Soon her brow was knotted with disapproval and she looked over my head and beyond my gaze to take her attentions away from what had become an imposing interrogation. I had been trying to make her understand that I had read about the controversy of the veil, that I knew what the topic was all about, but I was losing ground. Soon, my mother was approaching and I held my breath, dreading what would happen if she joined us.

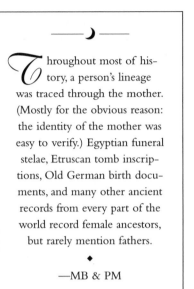

Throughout most of history, a person's lineage was traced through the mother. (Mostly for the obvious reason: the identity of the mother was easy to verify.) Egyptian funeral stelae, Etruscan tomb inscriptions, Old German birth documents, and many other ancient records from every part of the world record female ancestors, but rarely mention fathers.

♦

—MB & PM

I hoped nothing would be said that I would have to explain or retract; I stared at the dust coating the floor under my feet as I heard my mother asking about weather in the summer. "Wind," the woman replied, smiling. "Horrible storms from the desert bring in oceans of dust."

"Ah, the dust," my mother said. "And who cleans all the dust in a cathedral like this?"

The woman laughed. "Yes, that is quite a job! It takes many workers, men and women. There is no end to all the dust in Egypt!"

My mother laughed along. I was incredulous. What a coup! My mother was discussing housekeeping, the activity she avoided adamantly for most of her waking life (although she sometimes admitted that she did have nightmares about it). The truth is, I mused, that I have been compensating for her aversion to housework since I was seven. And so has my sister Anne. Our mother often chided us, her conscientious daughters, for succumbing to the tyranny of the housekeeper, whose goal in life is a perfectly clean house that no one wants to live in. Still, if I learned anything from my mother, I thought, it was to cultivate warmth and generosity in the face of overwhelming chaos, domestic and otherwise. There is no housekeeper you can pay, and no service you can hire, who will provide a genuine hospitality, my mother would say. Just as no known professional can provide the attention of a loving, worrying mother, a love as broad as the expanse of a warm blanket and narrow as the piercing vision of a hawk.

I looked at my mother standing alongside the Egyptian female guide; she resembled a sage from another epoch. The smooth plateaus between the wrinkles of her skin glowed like the worn alabaster columns that supported the dome above us, a forehead worn smooth after years of exposure to weather and living. Certainly she was in her element here. I took another look. I could see the guide was quite taken with this woman, my mother, the wise American grandmother.

Joyce Wilson is the editor of a Web page for poets, The Poetry Porch *(http://www.world.std.com/~jpwilson/).*

★

Daddy always said that Grandma Vera would go anywhere. "If someone said, 'Let's go,' she wouldn't ask where," he used to say, "she'd just say, 'Let me get my hat.'"

On a warm May day in 1964, queasy from sampling the tuna casseroles and chocolate cakes toted in by neighbors, I stand beside her open casket. Her ivory face, not quite the face I knew, sinks in puffs of pillowy satin, too fancy for her. I whisper, "Let's go, Vera."

The stories from my family past are stories of travel. Great events may fade from the mind, but memory fragments snag on a hardship of the road, a child's remark, a new view of the world. My mother, my grandmother, my great and great-great grandmothers were restless, curious, bold. From England to New England. From Keene, New Hampshire to Keene, Ohio. From east to west and back again.

From grandma and her maternal line, I inherited the urge to keep moving. For the women in my family, getting away from the ordinary provides impetus to wander. Travel exemplifies freedom.

—Vera Marie Badertscher, "Traveling Women"

CLAIRE TRISTRAM

✦ ✱ ✦

Camping with Lucy

*A one-word vocabulary opens worlds
for a mother and child.*

MY DAUGHTER LUCY BEGAN TO WALK ON OCTOBER 10, HER FIRST birthday, leaving me weepy and in awe of the huge journey she'd just taken from the sofa to her father's knee. The next morning, Lucy and I started off on a week-long camping trip. Our destination, the Pacific coast of Northern California, is one of my favorite places in the world. I wanted Lucy to like it as much as I do.

It wasn't Lucy's first outdoor experience. She first slept in a tent when she was six days old. An intrepid traveler, she doesn't seem to mind weather, bugs, or dirt. Not so her mom. Living outdoors doesn't come naturally to me. I crave plumbing. A telephone. A word processor. In many ways I'd planned this trip because I wanted my daughter to be more at home with the natural world than I am. But what continually surprises when traveling with my daughter is how much she is teaching me.

Lucy and I camp at Salt Point, four hours north of San Francisco, a place where sandstone cliffs and jagged rocks plunge straight into the sea. Occasionally a chunk of the highway falls into the sea, too, closing the route for days or weeks and making the area even more desolate than before. There's no town, only a lone general store where the closest thing to fresh produce is a can of chili. There's an occasional luxury home built on a bluff, a scattered hotel or two in the heavily-wooded hills, and the biggest Buddhist temple in the Western world, on a hilltop a few miles above our campsite. That's about it. It's mid-October. Definitely off-season, unless you're an abalone diver. We're the only people camping in the entire park.

None of these things matter to Lucy, of course. Her perspective on the world is far more immediate: whatever she can grab. Since I can't childproof the whole outdoors and don't want to confine her to a playpen, I've spent hours teaching her not to put things in her mouth that might choke her. We've developed a unique communication, she and I. Instead of shouting "No!" I yell "Ah-ah-ah!"—a sound, I'm embarrassed to admit, that was taught to me in dog obedience school for my Samoyed. It causes some confusion for my dog on this trip, but my baby responds immediately by dropping whatever is in her hand.

This afternoon, our first in camp, I don't need to say it. Lucy says it for me. She prowls around our site on all fours, earnestly searching out every small stone and shouting "Ah-ah-ah!" before crawling over and handing it to me with great ceremony.

Finally, the pile of stones next to me growing out of control, I pick Lucy up, put her in her carrier, put the dog on a leash, and take them both for a walk through the woods near our camp. Deer, quail, and what-just-might-be-a-fox cross our trail. I point to them with great excitement—my daughter is getting a great look at nature!—but it's unclear to me whether Lucy sees any of them, since she's busy looking at the ground for more stones.

Salt Point's only real beach is a small crescent of sand, Stump Beach, a few miles from our camp. On our third day, I hike down to the beach with Lucy, hoping to get out of the October wind. I've layered Lucy's clothes until she resembles a miniature fullback. The waves are rough and over fifteen feet high. It's peak abalone season, but no one is going into the water. A few glum divers sit on the beach in their wetsuits, complaining about the weather.

I've brought along a new pail and shovel for Lucy, which I set down in the sand next to her. She ignores them, preferring instead to play her own elaborate game with pieces of driftwood. She picks up a piece in each hand, throws them into the air simultaneously, and watches them earnestly as they drop. Again and again. After a while she crawls up into my lap and falls asleep under my down jacket. I decide to wait until she wakes up before moving her. The wind dies. The tide goes out. My arm goes to sleep. I wonder why the only reading material I've brought along on this trip is Sesame Street books for my daughter. I wonder if Big Bird is a man or a woman, and if Bert and Ernie are T.V's first same-sex marriage. I wonder if my daughter will ever wake up. Lucy wakes up and smiles.

On the fourth day we break camp, heading north on Route 1. The landscape grows more civilized almost immediately, as the craggy outcroppings of Salt Point smooth their way into flat farmland. At Stewart's Point General Store, we stop to get a book to read for me, and groceries for the both of us. I discover that Lucy has learned her first word. As we get out of the car, she shouts "Hi!" to a gruff old man in a battered cowboy hat. The wrinkles in his face realign themselves in a thousand smiles. Later on, behind us in line at the register, he gives us three cents so we can pay in exact change. "I knew I'd get rid of those pennies someplace," he says, looking only at my daughter.

Driving north again, we pass Sea Ranch, a huge development of luxury homes, before passing a real ranch, where a man is driving a tractor draped with two newly-butchered cattle. We pass a llama ranch, too, just in time to see two llamas mate. Lucy has fallen asleep in her car seat and I decide to keep driving, all the way to MacKerricher State Park, north of Fort Bragg, which is the largest town on this stretch of the California coast. The campsites are large, sunny, and a stone's throw away from a wide and wild beach.

Setting up camp is a time when I must keep Lucy confined somehow, since I'm too busy to watch her. I usually leave her in her car seat, or put her in the portable highchair I've brought, along with a few new toys for her to play with. After the tent is up I let her roam free, keeping her always in sight.

Today Lucy crawls to the next campsite, inexorably drawn towards the sound of another baby. The baby is dressed in white. She sits in her playpen like the Emperor of the Forbidden City, remote and wise and oh, so clean. My own daughter, whose favorite game in camp is to make mud by throwing dirt into our dog's water dish, looks something akin to an invading barbarian.

The other mother comes out of her mobile home, looking alarmed as my baby approaches hers.

"How old is she?" she asks in a voice that's just a little strained.

We learn our daughters were born within days of each other. I look at the two of them, looking at each other, one clean and civilized, the other dirty and wild, and I wonder what I'm teaching my daughter, and if she'll ever recover from it.

We visit Mendocino Village the next day, eight miles to the south, a coastal town so quaint that it's been the location of over three dozen feature films and countless television series and commercials. Even in mid-October the town is bursting with tourists.

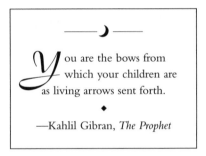

> *Y*ou are the bows from which your children are as living arrows sent forth.
>
> ♦
>
> —Kahlil Gibran, *The Prophet*

Lucy says "Hi" to a rough-looking woman in a flannel shirt and jeans. That's how we meet Mary, a woman who makes her living as a "water witcher," dousing for wells in the area. "My partner uses a coat hanger," she tells us. "I have a more complicated method, involving piano strings." Mary shows us her plumb bob, too, about the size of her thumbnail, dangling from a fine chain. She tells us that the plumb bob is connected with the spirit world, and will answer any question Mary asks it. She holds the plumb bob absently over my baby as we speak. It swings wildly. I'm afraid to ask Mary what it's saying.

Lucy's "hi" entices people to speak with us all day. It's a loud and lusty "hi," accompanied by a wave and a six-toothed smile. It's the perfect traveler's vocabulary, and all she needs to say—the people she says it to invariably take up the conversation from there. Lucy's "hi" stops a bent old man dead in his tracks. He looks at her in wonder, then tells her, "Look at you! Living for today! No thought for the future! Don't ever forget how to do that!" I want to ask how he got all of that out of my daughter's single-word vocabulary, but he's already walked by. Next Lucy stops a middle-aged couple with "Mendocino" written on matching sweatshirts, who are holding hands as they pass us. They both wave and say "hi" back again for several seconds, giddy with smiles, before moving on.

Then there's Larry Springer in Fort Bragg, Mendocino's work-ing-class neighbor to the north. Larry has a storefront on Redwood Avenue, where he runs the School of Common Sense Physics. He calls himself many things, including "Explorer of Radiant Energy," or simply "genius." In his eighties now, I get the feeling he is looking for a successor to take over his school.

Even in their oddness, Mary and Larry and all the people we meet in between all are somehow typical of this stretch of coast. Grizzled hippies and real estate agents, pot growers and cattle ranchers, water witchers and curmudgeons, and people just passing through all co-exist peacefully, and with a grudging respect for one another. Thanks to Lucy's one word, we get to meet quite a few of them.

The problems you have when traveling with small children al-ways have something to do with time, and what you'd rather be doing with it. You don't have time to read the book you've been meaning to read, because the baby won't nap when she's supposed to. You can't finish a meal, because she's getting too tired and needs to be nursed to sleep. You can't just relax and do nothing for a while, because she's demanding that you pay attention to her. You can't have fun, damn it, because your child just won't *cooperate*.

On the sixth day of our vacation, Lucy explodes. No more cute smiles—she screams constantly, a grating sound that leaves me on the edge of calling our vacation quits and going home. No more minding me, either. At our campsite she's grimly determined to put anything into her mouth—dirt, grass, bugs—that will cause her mother to leap up in horror to rescue her. No more napping on schedule—she stubbornly refuses to sleep that afternoon, despite my best efforts to get her to nod off so I can have some time to myself.

Finally, at four that afternoon, beaten down by my daughter's stubbornness and the sheer force of will, exhausted from trying to get her to sleep, I give up. I carry her to the beach, just over the dunes from our tent, and put her down on the sand.

She scrambles away from me as if she's driven to put as much distance between us as she can. Amazing how quickly she moves. I scramble after her.

Something happens then. A shift in the breeze and in my perception of the world. I discover that my daughter, who barely has taken her first step, can clamber over sea-rocks like the most nimble crab. My daughter, who knows only one word of English, can imitate perfectly the cry of a seagull, or a barking dog down the beach, or the drone of a passing airplane. My daughter, who is just a year old, can show me things about the world that are too subtle or too familiar for me to notice myself. She points to the barest whisper of a moon in the sky before I see it. To a dragonfly high above our heads. To a jet trail, lit up in the setting sun.

The next day it rains. Our vacation becomes a series of knotty problems to solve: how to keep Lucy warm and dry; how to keep the dog from tracking mud all over the back seat of the car; how to prepare and eat hot meals. This last problem we solve by giving up on the outdoor eating experience and going frequently to Denny's in Fort Bragg instead.

But nothing—not the rain, nor the mud, nor the sudden chill that tells me winter has finally come to the California coast—can get in the way of this shining memory: Lucy, on the beach at MacKerricher, at sunset, at the moment when I first felt her growing away from me.

Lucy Tristram, now two, inspired her travel-loving mom to write the book, Have Kid, Will Travel: 101 Survival Strategies for Vacationing with Your Baby. *Lucy lives in San Jose, California, with her mother Claire, a*

freelance writer, and her dad David, a computer programmer. Lucy's most re-
cent adventure was a week-long trip with her mom to Manhattan Island—
but that's another story.

★

Traveling with Lindy always brought new insights into the country visited. This was especially true in Egypt, where I learned that children,
above all, are the center of attention.

At five, Lindy was blonde, outgoing, and not afraid to speak her few
words of Arabic, a compelling combination for people drawn naturally
and delightfully to children. Cooks at restaurants invited her into their
kitchens to watch them prepare meals. Passersby stopped to say hello, and
to touch her hair. Old women and teenage girls gave her gifts of food and
coins—whatever they had to give. Even boys and men of all ages, first interested in a Western woman not wearing a scarf, forgot all about her in-
appropriately-clad mother when they spotted Lindy.

That she was an irresistible attraction is a commentary more on
Egyptians than on Lindy, cute as she was. My experience is that all children are adored in Egypt, which speaks volumes about the country, the
culture, and the compassion of a people who have a different understanding of the past and, it seems, a sophisticated sense of the future.

—Mary Fontaine, "Lindy in Egypt"

WENDY DUTTON

⋆ ⋆ ⋆

The Places I Went When My Mother Was Dying

Mother Nature comforts and heals.

THESE ARE THE PLACES I WENT WHEN MY MOTHER WAS DYING. Keep in mind she had cancer, so she was dying for a long time. Also keep in mind I have two small children, so the only way I could even begin to contemplate her death was to go deep into the wilderness. Some people think I'm crazy to camp alone in remote places, but for me there's no other kind of camping. I have never had any trouble. It's all in the approach.

My first such venture was to the Warner Mountains in the upper northwest corner of California. It was the first time I camped on national land, which means you can pretty much camp anywhere, though the best place is an old cowboy camp where you can find a ring of stones for a fireplace and the whole place littered with empty beer cans. I pictured the cowboys, getting sloshed, letting the cows run rampant. Giant cowpies were everywhere—as if there had been giant cows and giant cowboys who had to drink extra beers just to get a wilderness buzz.

I didn't exactly go alone. I went with Matthew. This was his vision quest spot. His mom led people on vision quests for a living. When he was thirteen, she brought Matthew along and he went

141

off like everyone else for three days of solitary camping—no food, just water. After that he didn't want to do any more vision quests and he developed a lifelong fetish for water, but he still liked to come to this place. It's true it was a totally alone place and therefore it had a kind of magic. Even the air there was different at such a high altitude. It sort of sparkled and had a watery taste.

I wanted to do a vision quest too, but I wanted to skip all the New Age stuff and cut right to the solitude. And so Matthew left me alone for a few days. I pictured him camped out somewhere above me, watching me gorging on granola and writing in my notebook. I even wrote at night. It was impossible to sleep with all those mosquitoes, divebombing in the moonlight. Even the mosquitoes were giant in those mountains.

On our last day we hiked so high I was dizzy. We got so high only the strongest wildflowers bloomed. "These are the Happy Mountains," Matthew informed me. "That's their real name." I skipped around like Maria in *The Sound of Music*. And then, suddenly, a view! We could see clear into Nevada. "That's the Surprise Valley," Matthew said. And it certainly was.

Whenever I went somewhere, I reported my travels to my mother. Though I write like a maniac, I never have been much of one for a journal. My mother was my journal. She was the person I told. Every time I returned from a trip, she asked me all about it over the phone. It was hard for her to imagine the far-outness of my destinations. She admired my affinity for aloneness, something she never liked.

Then she got cancer. It started out as breast cancer, her major fear. As we talked about it on the phone, and I felt my skin tingle, and my breasts ached. She told me this when I was about to leave for a trip to the dessert with Matthew. We decided to go anyway. What else was there to do?

This time Matthew didn't leave me alone, and it annoyed me, having him trip around the trickle of creek we had found, obstructing my view of nothingness. Finally he suggested we go on a rock collecting hike. He knew a trail that went to a place where there were crystals. "It's just a little bit up there," he said, "past that miner's shack."

I pictured us ambling along, picking up crystals. But "a little bit up" turned out to be several miles up, and there were no trees there, and it was sweltering hot, and our water jugs weighed us down. I felt like a kid, asking if we were there yet. But it was a long time before we were there. And when we reached the top, some-one had dynamited the hilltop and scavenged all the good crystals. We took some, but there was no joy in it.

On the way down, we began to quarrel. It wasn't just the long hike—it was my mom, or more precisely my panic about my mom. Suddenly everything seemed tragic, even my relationship with Matthew, because I quickly came to realize it would not sus-tain me through this crisis. Some people are good to be around when you are troubled, and some people are not. When you get to that up-in-the-air place, you can see that more clearly.

"My mom can't even help me with this," I worried. "My mom has cancer. Now we will talk about cancer. Boyfriends and camp-ing trips will seem trite by comparison. These crystals in my hand won't even matter."

In Indiana there are a lot of malls. In the winter people go to the malls to stay out of the cold. In the summer they go to the malls to stay out of the heat. You move from one air-conditioned place to the next. When I was there, we went from my mother's house to the hospital.

I read to my mom from the book I had read in the desert, *Rebecca*. I read to her through her first chemo treatment. She sat in a big "barber" chair while the toxic medicine pumped into her from an IV. Other patients were in other chairs, and behind them was all glass and a baby woods so green it glared. I am a good reader. I skipped over the descriptions and got right to the part where the man says, "You thought I loved Rebecca! I never loved Rebecca!" Everyone was listening, even the nurses.

At my mother's house, my mother said, "Do you want to see my scar?" But she was already unbuttoning her shirt. And she showed

me where her breast had been cut away. It was a deep pink line
with a white star at the end of it, and my breasts began to ache
again, looking at her.

"I brought you something," I murmured, and I pressed a crystal into her hand.

She fawned over it. She couldn't believe I had found it myself.

And then for a time the cancer went away. I took myself on a
trip to celebrate. I wanted to go up to the Oregon border where
the redwoods grow as big as houses. I wanted to get up against
that kind of size and tap into some good old-fashioned humility.

In those parts the redwoods grow right up to the coastline. The
constant fog and mist conceal the actual contour of the rolling
cliffs. Most days the ocean is just something you guess at. It's a
foggy netherland, floating out there somewhere, and the trees are
its towering protectors, stout as soldiers.

I went in the spring when there were hardly any people, and I
fell asleep on a hillside beneath a mammoth redwood. When I
woke, it had started to rain. It was still dark, so I moved to the car.
When I woke again, I realized my mistake: I had left my shoes out
in the rain.

I always had one big screw-up when I was camping—like forgetting my hat or forgetting matches or forgetting my knife.
Letting my shoes get wet, that was a big one. That's why I liked
camping alone; there was no one to scold me. Matthew and I had
split up, but I still appreciated him for showing me how to camp.
I appreciate that a lot actually.

Since my shoes were wet, I hiked barefoot in the redwoods. The
trails were so springy. The ferns gave off a lushness, casting huge
lacey patterns in the forest. It was still rainy and my feet went
numb. Sometimes I ran to keep warm. I ran from sunny spot to
sunny spot. I climbed over immense fallen trees. I spotted some
elk. I didn't spot any people. I was the freeest free in that forest.
Then the cancer came back.

In Indiana my mother said, "Are you ready to see my head?"

But she was already taking off her wig. Her head was bald and babyish, and she smiled, and then she cried because she thought I didn't like it.

The next day I stood in front of the mirror. Whenever I got to my mother's house, I looked in the mirror and thought I looked shaggy. My skin looked extra porous in her mirror, and my hair looked frayed like I had just come home after being out in the woods for a long long time. My mother came in and caught me cutting off a couple inches of my hair. "What are you doing?" she said.

The chemo didn't work. The cancer had spread to irretrievable places like the liver and the brain. The brain was the clincher. She called and told me that just before I was leaving on a trip to Mendocino for Thanksgiving. It was another escape plan, a solitude trip. I was glad to still go. I got deep into the Mendocino National Forest where there were no people whatsoever, just manzanita, pine, redwood, a shrinking lake, a noisy stream, falling rock. In the night I heard howling, and I liked it.

"Oh, I wish I could go with you," my mother had said; I felt as if she had. I felt it especially when I was driving out of the forest and along the Eel River, and I came across a bald eagle. He was sitting on a branch overlooking the river and also right next to the road. I pulled up right in front of him and got out of my truck. "You're supposed to fly away," I told him. I made like my arms were wings and flapped at him, but he held his perch boldly and let me study him. He had magnificent yellow talons, a snowy white cap, and a hooked yellow beak, dark brown body. "You're something," I told the bird. And still he wouldn't fly away. When I got back in the truck, I thought, "She's still with me."

My mother lay on the bed like she was offering herself to us, her body bloated and yellow, her head, bald and round, her expressions, so child-like. I memorized her body: her breasts not breasts at all, the stretchmarks flaring white across her belly, the bruises on her eyes, the spidery blue veins on her cinched feet. I knew she would never walk again. I knew it in an instant.

She babbled some. She spouted mathematical equations. Then she stopped talking. She had already stopped eating. They disconnected the IV, and that meant she had a couple days. But a couple days came and went, four days, five days. She lay there, staring wide-eyed, sometimes crying out. She did not die for nine days. Or was it ten?

I counted the trees outside her window. I wondered what it would all look like without snow. And when no one else was in the room, I said, "You're supposed to fly away." And I saw her in my mind's eye, flying away from me into a beautiful mountainous landscape, and then the mountains fell away, and it was just sky where she was going.

———— ☽ ————

When I turned my mother's ashes loose into the Seine's currents that dusk on Ile de la Cité, they crackled and sizzled as if with pleasure. It was a quiet evening and I knew my mother would be pleased to be there. After all, this peaceful park of Place Dauphine is a popular spot for lovers, young and old. My mother had been both.

◆

*—Diane LeBow,
"Dancing on the Seine"*

In the Spring I took my daughters to Big Sur. They were not so crazy about camping with me. That's because I didn't have a tent and had gotten in the habit of sleeping under the stars. My kids didn't like that. There are so many noises when you are sleeping on the ground. The world is alive all around you, and it can keep a kid awake, I'll tell you.

So I rented a cabin, and we woke up with the Big Sur Creek rushing at our feet. I woke before the girls and took an icy dip. The water was so cold it hurt. It had a metallic feeling, so silver and shining. I have wished many times since to start my day that way again.

I was starting to feel human again. That water could do that to you. But still it was a surprise. My mother had been dead three months, and I missed her terribly. Often I saw her face, her body, and I heard her weird dying words. And I wondered when I would remember her whole again as she had been before the cancer, my beautiful touchstone person, my mother.

That trip was all mother to me. But to my girls it was the water, the cliffs, getting naked, and running around crazily. Naturally I wanted to tell my mother about it, how beautiful my girls had looked when they rose and found me in the creek. "What are you doing in the *water*?" they squealed.

"Breathing deeply," I replied, but they were already rushing out to meet me.

Wendy Dutton has published work in The Threepenny Review, Hip Mama, The Single Mother's Companion, *and* Farmer's Market. *She lives in Oakland, California, with her two daughters, where she gardens for a living.*

★

Death always comes too early or too late.

—English proverb

KYLE E. MCHUGH

* * *

A Hand in the Darkness

A mother and daughter cope with blindness.

THE CHRISTMAS SEASON OF 1981 WAS NO HOLIDAY FOR ME. THE day after Thanksgiving I had awakened blind in one eye, the result of diabetic retinopathy. Doctors told me that it was only a matter of time before I would lose the vision in the other eye as well. I had recently left Boston University with one year remaining, hoping to repair my damaged eyes with laser surgery. Now, back in my parents' home in Pennsylvania, I believed I had no future and that any worthwhile living had ended.

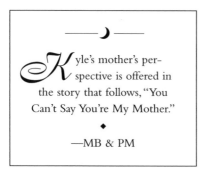

Kyle's mother's perspective is offered in the story that follows, "You Can't Say You're My Mother."

◆

—MB & PM

For days I lay in the bed in my old bedroom, feeling hopeless and incapable of the simplest task. As each day passed, I watched the details of the world fade into a blur, knowing that soon it would all disappear into a cavernous darkness.

My mother kept me alive during those days when my only purpose seemed to be to watch myself deteriorate. She made me special meals and cut my food, helped me find the right color clothes if I ever dared to dress, and rubbed my back through hours of inactivity.

Trying to maintain some semblance of Christmas, my mother bought a tree and shopped for presents. As she hung the lights and the fragile glass ornaments on the tree, she thought of all the years when she and I had done it together, reminiscing about past Christmases and laughing at our own foibles. Now, she had no idea whether I would even be able to make out the shape of the tree, or the brightly colored lights that studded its branches.

One afternoon my mother went out to the mall, feeling little Christmas spirit as she shopped for last minute gifts. I remained in bed, half listening to the television that droned on in my bedroom.

A few hours later, I heard her return. She burst into my bedroom, still wearing her coat, and sat on the edge of my bed. She smelled of the cold, crisp air outside and had tiny bits of snow melted on her collar. From one of her bags she excitedly withdrew a package. "I found you the greatest thing!" she said enthusiastically as she opened the box. Inside was a small silver cube with a large button on top. She pressed the button and a steady male voice announced, "It's 4:36 p.m."

She watched for my reaction, placing my hands on the button. When I pressed it, it announced the time again in the same clear voice.

"Where did you find it? " I asked, actually smiling for the first time in days.

"I got it at Radio Shack," she said. "I thought you might like it."

I sat up in bed and inspected the clock with my hands. My mother read me the instructions, explaining that I could make it announce the time on the hour if I wished.

It was then that I realized—for the first time since the start of my impending blindness—that I could do something independently. It struck me how totally helpless I had been, not even able to know what time it was without asking for assistance. I cleared a space on the table next to my bed and put the clock there.

In the weeks that followed, my vision deteriorated and so did my spirit. I could not imagine being competent at anything ever again, much less capable of caring for myself. I was destined to spend the rest of my life in my parents' home, far from the life in Boston I had adored.

On one rare occasion, I left the safety of my bedroom and inched my way downstairs. I felt along the walls, heading toward the kitchen. Before I reached the door, however, I heard my mother crying inside. She was pleading with God, angry that he had destroyed the life of her child. How could he have taken away a life so full of hope and promise? Tears fell on my nightgown as I turned and climbed the stairs back to my bedroom. Not only had my life ended, but my mother's had as well, for I knew that she would sacrifice most of her time and energy to care for me, doing her best to put joy back in my life. If that meant giving up her career as a writer, her many friends, and her frequent travel, I was sure that she would do it. I sat on the edge of my bed and abandoned my own self-pity for the moment.

Although I had no future, I could not condemn my own mother to a life of servitude. My blindness was a freak of nature. My mother's sacrifice would be one of pure love. I went to the telephone and called the Pennsylvania rehabilitation program for the blind. I had met with their representatives earlier, at a time when I was too hopeless to be encouraged by their words. This

---

> nna watched her daughter fall asleep. The palsy tremors ceased, Karen's limbs were in repose. "How still you are," she whispered. "So quiet when you sleep." Anna rubbed the mosquito bites then patted her daughter's arms. "Such funny arms. Arms that have never held a man. Arms that cannot even hug your mother." She took the soft hem of her robe and wiped the spittle from her daughter's chin.
>
> ◆
>
> —Meta E. Lee, "My Child"

time, I was prepared to listen. When I told my mother that I was ready to begin living again, she seized the opportunity to help me. While I had occupied my time watching my world fade away, she had been forced to stand by helplessly and watch. Now she could be a part of my recovery. Since I had always loved to read, we decided that reading Braille must be my first priority.

It had never looked very difficult when I had seen blind people reading Braille in the movies, their fingers skimming lightly along the pages. Perhaps I could do that.

My mother ordered a book of Braille instruction, with raised dots on one side and print on the other. As I struggled to distinguish the confusion of meaningless lumps beneath my fingers, my mother taught herself to sight-read the configuration of the dots. She spent hours with me, practicing the frustrating task of training my fingers and my mind to recognize the various letters. She made me excited about the joy of learning something new, despite my frequent desire to abandon the effort as hopeless.

As she had when I was a child learning to read for the first time, she came up with creative ways to help me practice my reading. At that time, we were still spending hours in the waiting rooms of eye doctors, pursuing the slightest chance of a magical cure. As we sat next to each other in overcrowded hospital hallways and doctor's offices, my mother would grasp my hand and place it on her own. Slowly, she would tap out Braille messages in my hand, converting the raised dots to a sort of Morse code.

I loved the stories my mother told me in those days. She always made me laugh by describing the fat and forlorn Philadelphians in the waiting room with us, or telling me jokes with punch lines enhanced by my struggle to decipher them. The words I grew to know the best, however, were, "I love you."

My parents hired a private tutor to begin my mobility training before I entered the rehab center. As I wandered aimlessly down the street, waving my white cane in front of me, my mother tagged along, making careful note of the instructor's words. She could feel how terrified I was to step into the dark space before me, unsure of what dangers might lay ahead. While her being there added little confidence to my walking, I knew that she would be there to pick me up if I fell down.

As the weeks progressed, my mother delighted at my slightest progress. She listened with interest as I introduced her to my new world, and cried with me over seemingly insurmountable obstacles.

I was moving forward, and she was right by my side.

By the spring I was ready and anxious to return to Boston. As I packed up my possessions, I was far too excited about returning to a productive life to fear the consequences. My mother had helped me find a beautiful apartment in the heart of the city. She shopped with me to find suitable furniture and equipment to stock the kitchen, and made beautiful curtains for the bedroom and living room.

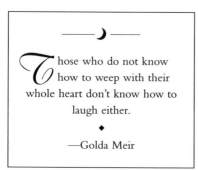

Those who do not know how to weep with their whole heart don't know how to laugh either.

◆

—Golda Meir

I don't know how we survived the actual move, for it entailed several sleepless nights, an overpowering rainstorm, and movers who failed to arrive with my furniture. But some inner core of strength and determination held us up. We even found ourselves laughing at the absurdity of the whole disastrous situation. Once the boxes had arrived, my mother helped me put everything in its place. She cleaned shelves before lining them with paper, ran to the hardware store to buy a hammer and nails to hang pictures on the wall and hung the new drapes at the window.

Once the furniture was in place, my mother patiently converted my possessions to those of a blind person. She sewed Braille tags into my clothes to indicate their color and labeled my voluminous files with similar tags. She helped me organize my shoes so that I didn't confuse the black ones with the blue ones, and sorted the food in my freezer into distinct sections. Together we took endless walks around my neighborhood to acquaint me with the various twists and turns of the streets.

Finally, the day arrived when my mother had to return to Pennsylvania, my father, and her own life. As she hugged me for the last time, I panicked, wondering what on earth I was doing there.

"I don't know if I can do this," I cried.

She put her suitcase down and hugged me again.

"Then you can always come home," she said.

I know that it was just as hard for her to leave as it had been for me to let her go. We had shared so much in the preceding months, such tragedy and triumph. She had watched me grow up all over again and now she had to let me go for the second time. When she had sent me off to college many years before, we both had known I would make it. But now, the future was a mystery.

My mother has become an even closer friend in the years that have followed. She had me written up in a magazine when I got a job as an aide to a state senator, cheered louder than anyone when I graduated from a Master's program at Harvard and even traveled with me as my assistant on a consulting job I had in Kiev. She brags about me to anyone who will listen, often making me sound a bit too super-human. Yet, she never gives herself credit for inspiring my spirit and lighting the spark within me that makes me want to go on. Perhaps she doesn't realize that she is a part of every one of my accomplishments.

Maybe that's just part of being a mother.

Kyle E. McHugh is a consultant in international health care who has worked in a psychiatric asylum in England, for a member of Parliament in Northern Ireland, for the homeless in Germany, and conducted an evaluation of the health care system in Ukraine. She lives in Boston and is the first blind woman to receive a Mid-Career Master of Public Administration degree from Harvard's Kennedy School of Government.

*

Your hands! I love your hands! Those blue bulgy veins you think are "un-attractive" are really the blue streams of the high country. They are your ways of worshiping as you work in the earth, your version of the shaping The Great Spirit does, as you are shaped in return. And so are the very life forces shaped as they work through you, learning in their turn, and, as it has taken time for this round, this partnership to be formed, so have your hands evolved. It has taken time for them to be distilled, like wine, and to grow, like the roots of trees. Look at the bark of a stone pine or the twisting branches of a madrone. Look at your hands again, and see through my eyes: by God! they have seen all weathers! A baby's hand might be freshly-minted and have its own beauty, but it has no soul, for it takes time for a canyon, or a pair of hands, to grow a soul.

I see you shining through the skin of your hands like the sun inside the leaves of your apple tree.

—Geoffrey Brown, *Road of the Heart Cave*

MARY MCHUGH

You Can't Say You're
My Mother

Undercover mom fights for her daughter's survival.

THE MINUTE WE LAND AT BORIS POL AIRPORT IN KIEV, MY daughter Kyle and I are rushed into an ambulance. We have absolutely no need of one, but here we are in a strange van with a stretcher, a red cross on the window, and a wild-haired man in a white coat trying to lift Kyle with her bandaged leg into the vehicle. He's chattering away in Ukrainian, but since our Ukrainian is limited to "Hello," "Goodbye," and "Do you speak English?" we have no idea what he is saying.

We are in Kiev so Kyle can write a report on health care in Ukraine for the World Institute on Disability. My daughter lost her sight 14 years ago when she was 22

Mary's daughter's perspective is offered in the preceding story, "A Hand in the Darkness," by Kyle E. McHugh.

♦

—MB & PM

because of diabetic retinopathy, but nothing stops her. After she became blind, she packed her things, moved to an apartment in Boston, found a job with a state senator, earned a mid-career

Masters at Harvard and now runs her own health care and social services consulting business.

When Kyle lost her sight, I thought I would never laugh or be happy again. It took a year for her to become blind. Doctors had always assured me that laser treatments would save her vision. Instead, after months of treatment at Columbia Presbyterian's Harkness Pavilion in New York, she developed glaucoma and lost every bit of her vision. They weren't able to save one small glimmer of light.

As her sight slowly faded away, she lay in bed—it was Christmas time—and I didn't know how to help her. You always think there is something you can do to help your child, something to fix whatever is wrong. But sometimes you can't.

So I rubbed her back, taught her Braille, bought her a talking clock, did what I could. Then one day she said, "I can't see your face anymore."

A month after she became blind, she heard me crying in the kitchen. She had felt her way down the stairs from her bedroom and sat there quietly as I raged at God, at life, at fate for blinding my daughter. I didn't know she was there and I yelled, howled, moaned. This is very unlike me. I am descended from frozen Scots who don't express anguish or joy aloud. Stiff upper lip was the rule I grew up with, but now I sobbed for my child.

Kyle climbed the stairs back to her room and called the center for the rehabilitation of the blind. She made an appointment to get help, and from that time on, my Kyle learned to walk with a cane, to take the subway alone, to read Braille, to improvise. She went back to Boston and a life.

Now, Kyle just gets on planes and goes—to England to work in a psychiatric hospital, to Belfast to work for a member of the British Parliament, to Germany to work in a homeless shelter. Her blindness bothers her not at all.

"Once you stop thinking like a sighted person, it's O.K.," she says. "It's all figuring out how to get from here to there without bumping into the furniture."

She usually travels alone, but this time she thought I might come in handy as her sighted guide. We would be in Kiev for a month.

"Don't expect to be comfortable," she said. "And there's one other thing, Mom. You can't say you're my mother on this trip. I'll be working as a professional consultant and I don't want to tell people I'm with my 'mommy.' People tend to turn to you anyway when we're together because I'm blind, so this time, I'll introduce you as 'Mary, my assistant.' Is that O.K. with you?"

"Sure," I said. "That's fine."

But I had no idea how hard it would be to lose my last name, my identity as a writer, and especially my role as Kyle's mother.

My husband Earl warned me that Kyle could have an insulin reaction and die because medical help is almost nonexistent in Ukraine. He tells me about a woman who came back from Kiev with a serious infection after being treated for appendicitis there. But he's been a pessimist all his life, so I don't listen. Anyway, nothing is going to happen to my daughter while I'm around.

As we sit in the ambulance totally confused, not knowing what to expect, a solemn young soldier or policeman or ex-KGB man suddenly appears and takes our passports. That's it, we think. We're here for life, about to be locked up in some mental hospital. I'll never see my husband or older daughter Karen again. My three grandsons will grow up without me. But the soldier returns with a polite, English-speaking man who pronounces each word carefully.

"Excuse me. You are in need of medical attention?"

"No!" we say.

Kyle explains that she has had recent knee surgery and that is why we have a wheelchair with us, but we don't need a doctor. We tell him we have arranged to meet a man named Nikolai, who will take us to our apartment.

The young man leads me to a luggage area where I easily find our bags sitting on the cement floor. No carousels, just a cement floor, but I have never found my luggage more easily in any other country. He takes them to the ambulance and that's the extent of the customs interrogation, security check, weapons search, questions on political correctness, and red tape we were expecting.

We zoom around to the front of the airport and our wild-haired companion runs into the terminal and returns with Nikolai, a large, smiling Ukrainian who had been searching for us.

"Hallo," he says. "Where you was?"

We explain.

"You are sisters, no?" Nikolai asks.

Kyle and I hesitate and then say yes.

Kyle mutters, "One of us looks a lot different than I remembered."

I'm 60 and thrilled to be mistaken for her sister.

We drive to the first apartment of four we would live in before finding the right one. As we speed along the excellent highway, I describe what I see to Kyle. Acres of apartment buildings, run-down and seedy, like the housing projects in our cities. Stores with nothing in them. Buses crammed with people squashed against the windows. A towering silver statue of a woman holding a sword and shield—the symbol of the motherland—high on a hill above the city. The Dnieper River which divides Kiev into a right and left bank. Near the statue the golden domes of Lavra, monastery of the caves, gleam in the afternoon sunlight.

Nikolai promises Kyle that he will be her protector, her guardian angel, while we are in Kiev.

"I arrange for you appointment at school for deaf-mute children, factory for blind workers. I help you with whatever you need. Just ask."

We park at the back of an apartment building in the Pechersk section of Kiev on the right bank and get out of the car. Kyle stops in dismay inside the building. Four steep flights of stairs lead to our flat.

"We need to find another apartment, Nikolai," she says. "I had surgery a month ago and I cannot do this. I made that clear when I arranged for the flat."

"You will become stronger," Nikolai says.

"No, Nikolai," Kyle says. "I could damage my knee permanently if I abuse it now."

"OK, OK," he says. "We stay here tonight and move in the morning. If you don't like next flat, I find you another and another. Don't worry."

Painfully, step by step, Kyle climbs the four flights of stairs to be greeted with a hug by Tamara, a sweet, gold-toothed woman in her seventies, a veteran of World War II. She opens the door to a spotless, cozy apartment. Flowered paper on the ceiling. Oriental rugs on the wall to keep out the cold. A TV tuned to a soap opera. China figurines, paintings, photographs of a man and two little boys. This is completely different from the bare-bones apartment I had been expecting.

Tamara leads us to her kitchen for oniony potatoes, fried eggs, the best bread I've ever eaten, and tea. I forget cholesterol, calories, and fat and stuff myself with this feast. (I end up losing eight pounds on a diet of butter, eggs, peanut butter, bread, sour cream, and Fig Newtons.)

Kyle goes into the bedroom to give herself a booster shot of insulin. Her blood sugar is high because of jet lag. She gives herself too much; a few minutes later, I find her unconscious. I try giving her a glucose tablet, but it's no use. She is not moving or responding. I pray she will wake up, say something to me, but I know she can't. I have seen her like this many times before.

My husband's warning echoes in my head. An insulin reaction in a country where the hospitals have no bandages, antibiotics, syringes, things we take for granted. When Kyle has a reaction at home, paramedics come, start a glucose IV, take her to the hospital, and within half an hour she is fine. But in Kiev, I don't know what to expect. Would they come? Would they know what to do? Would they have glucose? Would Kyle die here? And it will be all my fault. I shouldn't have let her come.

I am terrified but not paralyzed.

"Nikolai," I say. "Kyle has to get to the hospital. She's having an insulin reaction and needs glucose immediately."

"No hospital," Nikolai says. "They come here. They fix."

He calls a doctor. Tamara phones three times in ten minutes. Often, they tell me, a doctor does not come for hours. I sit there waiting beside my unconscious daughter, looking at that lovely face, remembering her as a little girl before the diabetes hit when she was six—before she had to have a shot of insulin every day, before she could have reactions.

Tamara waits beside me, her hand on mine, tears in her eyes. She has seen someone die of an insulin reaction. I hug her and try to reassure her with gestures and facial expressions, since she speaks no English. We wait. We are lucky. Within twenty minutes a dark-haired, weary doctor and two assistants arrive, all wearing white coats. They open a bag and take out a huge glass syringe, something from the nineteenth century, something for horses, and I think, "They could kill her."

> *A*fter twenty years of encouraging my son's independence, suddenly I found myself obsessed with his safety, worrying when he went out with friends for a beer, or when he exhausted himself on the basketball courts. Food intake, exercise, a head cold—for the diabetic, all these things affect insulin dosage in mysterious and difficult to calculate ways.
>
> ◆
>
> —Pamela Michael, "Apron Strings," *Travelers' Tales: Food*

"Nikolai," I say. "She needs glucose. Please she must go to the hospital."

"They know what they are doing," Nikolai says. "Don't worry."

I'm not at all sure they know what they are doing, but I watch them gently, carefully inject something into Kyle's arm. In less than a minute she opens her eyes.

"Kyle," I say, "You're in Kiev. You had a reaction. The doctor is here and they're giving you glucose. Are you O.K.?"

She smiles at me. "I'm sorry," she says. "You must be so worried."

My whole body relaxes. She's all right. She has survived an insulin reaction in Ukraine. If we can get through that, we can get through anything.

Then she says, "Did you give them my syringe? They re-use theirs."

Oh dear God, I think. She could get AIDS. My husband was right.

"No," I say.

"It's all right," she says. "I had a tetanus shot before I came."

That doesn't solve AIDS, but I block it out. I do that a lot with Kyle. I have to believe everything will be all right. When she went to Boston to live alone, I had to let her go, to believe she could live alone, that she wouldn't be killed by a car or on a subway, that she could cook and survive and have a life as a blind person. And she did.

When she traveled to Europe alone, I had to believe she could get from planes to metros to buses to taxis alone, and she did. When her kidneys failed, I had to believe she would get another one when mine proved not good enough to give her. And she did get one from an accident victim.

I know she can do anything she sets her mind to, but sometimes my heart is in my mouth. I stifle all the "Be carefuls," the "Are you sure you can do thats?" the "Is it safe?" It's hard, but I had to let her fly or I would have kept her from having a life.

The kind doctor and his silent assistants stay about ten minutes, waiting to be sure she is all right and then apologize for leaving—they still have many calls to make. There is no charge, they say.

I grab the doctor's hand and stammer out the Ukrainian word for thank you. He smiles a small, tight smile, pats my hand and leaves.

Crisis over, we share soup, bread, cheese, and apples with the kind Tamara. My apprehensions begin to fade a little, lulled by her pampering and her cozy apartment. Later, cuddled together, Kyle and I fall asleep under duvet covers over warm blankets. Tomorrow, Kiev awaits.

Mary McHugh is the author of Special Siblings: Growing Up With a Brother or Sister With a Disability. *She also has written six other books, and has been published in* The New York Times, Good Housekeeping, *and* Travel Holiday.

*

When the villagers first called out to me "*Namaste* Mother," I was put

off. "I'm not your mother!" I grumbled to myself. But after ten days on
the trail, the journey over, I begin to dream about the *chautaara*—rest-
stops—the best place on the trail to connect with other Nepali travelers, one to one.

You sit down, resting your pack on the high wall that encircles the
pipal tree—tired—and they are tired too. They sit on their haunches and
smoke. You mop your neck and put suntan lotion, SPF 15, on your nose.
They all want a dab, and you pass it around. They offer you a slice of
melon. Maybe there's even another breathless old woman with white hair
and lines in her face, an *aamaa* like you. She gives you a great, deep laugh
and asks how old you are. When you finally get up to move on, you each
bow your head towards the other, and this time, "*Namaste* Mother,"
sounds exactly right.

—Virginia Barton Brownback, "Nepal"

BARBARA WILDER

✦ ✦ ✦

The Beat of Aeonian Drums

The mother-goddess appears
in the English countryside.

THE FALL MORNING WAS COOL AND CRISP. FOR THE FIRST TIME since I'd arrived the sky was cloudless. I walked past an excavation of Roman ruins overgrown with grass and wild flowers. Though tempted to stop and explore, I resisted the impulse and continued on. But after several minutes I became aware of a strange disquieting feeling the ruins had stirred in me. In Italy I had always found the stumbled-upon ruins friendly, almost whimsical, but here they seemed out of place. Perhaps it was just the want of the Mediterranean sun enhancing the ancient stone with its romantic glow. But it was more. The earth seemed almost as if it were rebelling against the stern bridle of Roman orderliness, the land straining against the harness of the overlord. England, always considered so proper, so tamed, was sending signals of a very different kind here in Dorset. I'd been aware since my arrival a week ago of an almost pagan sensibility in the rural people here. Now, as I pressed on toward my destination, I was beginning to see a parallel between the ancient ways of the people and the spirit of the ground itself.

This morning I had planned to drive to the village of Cerne Abbas to see the Neolithic giant carved into a hillside there, but when I mentioned my plans to the proprietress of my bed and breakfast, she said that if I were truly interested in the prehistoric I should go directly to the Maumbury Rings. I have a rather stubborn nature and usually put off other people's suggestions until I've exhausted my own agenda, but there was something in her look when she shoved the quickly scrawled directions into my hand that made me follow her dictate without hesitation.

Soon I had left the Roman ruins behind. Passing the train station and the constabulary brought me abruptly back to the twentieth century. But not for long. After walking another half a city block there it was looming before me: a huge ring of earth at least thirty feet high and three hundred feet long that was completely overgrown with the ever-present wild English grass. It was the quintessential front lawn, and the eight-year-old girl in me rose up, giggling with anticipation. I wanted to run into that Ring and roll down its grassy slopes, but my spontaneity was frustrated by a rusted turnstile gate. The latch was unfamiliar to me, and I had to fiddle with it for several seconds. When I had finally released it and moved through the gate, my enthusiasm was muted by an overwhelming sense of awe. I wasn't more than three feet closer to the grand monument, but I was in another world and time. I walked slowly to the historical plaque at the north entrance and read, "Originally, a great stone henge stood in the south entrance, but it was removed by the Romans, who converted the prehistoric religious site into an amphitheater for their games and gladiatorial combats."

Later that day I was to learn that in 1705, a young woman named Mary Channing was hanged here in the presence of ten thousand people for the crime of murdering her husband, though there was neither motive nor evidence upon which to base the conviction. In fact, there was strong evidence that she was innocent. Her pregnant condition at the time of the trial won her a six month reprieve, but once the baby was born, the sentence was carried out. In 1705, public executions of women were still immensely fashionable and cause for celebration. Most often the crime was witchcraft, in other words, activities that threatened the preeminence of the Christian God. So, any crime by a woman against a man was considered worthy of great public spectacle, as evidenced by the gathering of ten thousand to watch the hanging of the new mother, Mary Channing.

But as I turned from the historical plaque and looked across the grassy path to the entrance of the Rings I was ignorant of Mary Channing's story. I knew only that this was a prehistoric henge monument that had been transformed by the Romans for their own particular form of barbarism.

Reading the plaque momentarily reestablished my status here as a tourist, and I began my ascent with a confident stride. But as I got closer my steps became more halting, and when I stepped up to the entryway the awe I had felt initially reasserted itself, leaving me immobilized before a large grass bowl the size of a football field. The area where the bleachers stood during the Roman era, was now eroded and overgrown with a thick green carpet rising thirty or forty feet

The old culture also survives in modern Orkney in households where weddings are set for days when the moon is waxing and the tides flowing. The pagan world is radiant in the farm and agricultural shows of August. Goddess emblems are found on the handsome cast-iron house signs with deer, trees, snakes, and pigs hovering over the numerals.

◆

—Emily Hiestand, *The Very Rich Hours: Travels in Orkney, Belize, the Everglades, and Greece*

and obliterating from view everything but the crystal blue canopy of sky. Nothing, neither animate nor inanimate, disturbed the pristine landscape until I, a lone red-haired woman in Levis, finally reassembled my faculties and made my way across the threshold.

At that moment all sounds from the outside world ceased, replaced by a hollow swirling sound of silence which grew increasingly intense the farther into the Rings I went. Each step seemed to swathe me in another layer of the Rings' magic. And when, at last, I arrived at the center, I knew I had entered the vortex of something very ancient and extremely powerful.

Slowly I turned on this center point, gathering in all that my eyes could accommodate, eventually returning to my starting position. The silence rose to a crescendo that forced me down toward the ground until I was seated cross-legged in the organic navel of the place.

The grass was still dew-wet; it quickly soaked through my jeans. I wondered if I should meditate, but before I could finish the thought a dark, ultra-violet mist rose from the depths of the ground beneath me and enveloped the entire space. Then transparent figures in the deepest shades of vermilion began to bleed through the mist, projected against the walls of the Rings, flickering like images in an early silent film.

Women covered in red paint, some wearing deer heads with antlers, danced around open pits of fire, holding elaborately carved wooden wands. They raised them above their heads, then with precise and powerful movements lowered them to the ground. Drummers sat in niches carved into the sides of the Rings high above the dancers. Everyone and everything was drenched in red paint, or blood. The sound of the drumming grew louder and louder. Everyone and everything was feminine, the dancers, the drummers, the great priest. The blood dripped off them and clung to them. And in their faces I saw a fierceness unequaled in any painting or sculpture or photograph of any human in any society.

I witnessed this all with the full knowledge that I was being allowed to view the gravest, most sacred rite of a civilization whose memory had been buried for thousands of years when the Romans arrived on this soil. A civilization so old that the most ancient Druids had heard only vague whispers of its existence.

Perhaps minutes had passed, or hours, or seconds, when the women, the priests, the drummers and dancers, the blood and the dark violet mist faded back into the deep recesses of the ancient Rings leaving me in the Maumbury Rings of twentieth century Dorchester. I looked at my watch. Ten thirty-five. Only five minutes, but five minutes in another millennium. But which one?

How long ago had these fierce and potent women ruled the world? Before the Romans? Definitely. Before the Druids? Yes. Before the Celtic Druids, at any rate. Were there Druids before the Celts? Yes, but an earlier form. The Celtic Druids evolved from a much older order in an era when the priests and shamans were all women; when the only thing that could maintain the human race in an untamed wilderness world was the savage ferocity of the feminine energy fighting for the survival of the brood she nurtured. A time when blood is what linked humans to the gods, and the Great Goddess was mother of all, of birth and death, bleeding periodically, queen of the fields and the caves, guide from the life on earth to the life after death. Wolf woman, fiercely competing with the Titans (floods, ice ages, ferocious beasts, droughts, heat, starvation, death in childbirth, infant death, disease) for the continuance of her issue. Anything and everything was sacrificed to make life on earth work.

I stood up and stretched my legs. Nothing stirred across the open green, not a bird nor a field mouse, just the grass under the tent of sky. But now I knew differently. I knew the insistent pounding of aeonian drummers resided somewhere beneath the blood-soaked layers of witch hunts and Roman centurions. And I was also in-

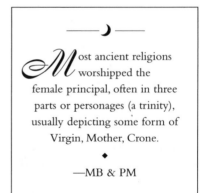

Most ancient religions worshipped the female principal, often in three parts or personages (a trinity), usually depicting some form of Virgin, Mother, Crone.

♦

—MB & PM

tensely aware that this antediluvian rhythm would not cease as long as the earth continued to orbit the sun. Because this was the pulse of the feminine energy, articulated by the earliest peoples of our race, held in this cup of earth, this holy grail.

As I walked up to the threshold of the south entrance to leave, I crossed paths with a young mother and her vivacious two-year-old son. He ran ahead of her through the portal where the ancient henge had stood. He squealed with delight as he toddled down the

gently sloping hill into the Rings and threw himself face first onto
the damp grass. I stood with his mother watching him rush into
this great earthen womb.

"This is a wonderful place for children," I said.

"Oh, yes. Lovely," she said.

Could she feel the power here? Had she seen the dancers and
the drummers and the festival of blood? Perhaps. Perhaps when she
was a child. Perhaps that's why she brought her child here now,
while he was still receptive to the magic she remembered only in
her dreams.

*Barbara Wilder is a writer and teacher, who worked for twenty years in Los
Angeles in the motion picture industry as a screenwriter and associate producer. She now resides with her poet husband in Boulder, Colorado where she
teaches writing at the Naropa Institute and a workshop, "Money is Love."*

★

Sometimes people go on pilgrimages to sacred sites, but such intense experiences are not the real life of religion, which must take place every day.
To make the connection with long-ago worshipers, many contemporary
women create altars in their homes or at community centers. They place
on them images, symbols, and objects once sacred to a particular deity,
such as paintings of a lunar crescent for the Moon Goddess
Artemis/Diana. Often they will elaborate the altar with photographs and
other tokens of their own lives. Having created a personal link to the
original worship and mythology, they then perform their own ceremonies, using poetry, dance, or other forms of observance.

And they talk. They allow the sacred power of the Goddess to open
up some aspects of their lives, some area where they seek healing, or in-
spiration, or understanding. Unlike the institutional religions most of us
know from childhood, with their complex rites and strict tradition, these
loose rituals work directly on the lives of the people doing them.

—Rachel Pollack, "Homemade Rituals of the Goddess," *Orion*

SUSAN ZWINGER

✶ ✶ ✶

Whacked Upside the Soul

And the child shall lead the mother
to Mother Earth.

SECONDS AFTER I CLIMB DOWN THE SIX-FOOT ROOTS OF A BEACHED
log, a high tide wave from the Pacific Ocean explodes nearby. The
water shoots forty feet into the air, surging under the log pile and
foaming down the other side of the spit. I cower like a small vole,
unprepared for the fear that shoots up from the soles of my feet.

All in a naturalist's day's work.

I am driven to write about the natural world because I love it
and because I want to heighten Americans' awareness of it. To
me, it is a national tragedy that as we've become more urban, our
connections to the wilderness—to the source of all life, food,
medicines, spiritual nourishment, play and exploration—are
being forgotten.

I go far out into places where human beings are small and in-
significant to sense my place in them. I go out most often alone,
seeking closeness to a very elemental power. I sit near the thun-
dering waves in winter at the highest of high tides in the Pacific. I
watch the roaring black water cascading down the precipitous
black stone on a mountaintop in Alaska. I see the unfamiliar immense expanses, hoping that they will slam into my consciousness
as segments of the Earth's crust slam into one another. My writing

is the faulting and uplift, the earthquake and vulcanism that result from such interface.

I go out into the humble, the intimate, the subtle wild places closer to home. In a nearby forest, within a few square feet I find hundreds of moss and lichen and liverwort. Whenever I feel confined or blue, I go out to watch the world inventing itself anew. The human eye is a peculiar organism—at first it sees nothing, then a little, and then such an abundance that I lose all sense of my tiny self and am swept into the wondrous infinity of life.

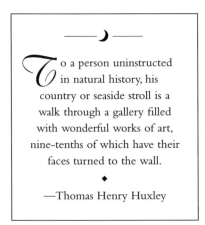

To a person uninstructed in natural history, his country or seaside stroll is a walk through a gallery filled with wonderful works of art, nine-tenths of which have their faces turned to the wall.

♦

—Thomas Henry Huxley

I am drawn, as my mother is, to the critical edges of life, be they warm test tubes of tidal pools or harsh expanses of Arctic tundra. Whenever I need a good whack upside the soul, I go to Earth's extremes and study the politics of survival. I love to imagine life beginning in these highly improbable conditions, in difficult crevices of rock and sea. I imagine myself a part of those amino acids which so suddenly glowed, organized, and slithered out of the mud pool.

I find wildness without even leaving home. The night sky above my apartment is filled with so many connect-the-dot mythological creatures and heavenly bodies that I cannot help but feel closer to the source of all life. The human urge to name, to categorize, to sort and explain falls away, and I gaze upward with a primitive awe.

I go out into the wilderness to be shocked, to be surprised into alertness. Once, walking alone in Alaska's Denali National Park, head down, unaware of my surroundings, I was terrified by what sounded like the sudden roar of a locomotive. A nine-foot wall of steely water burst toward me down a dry river channel. It was bizarre to watch the snout of a river move toward me like a train. High enough alongside its path, I was safe to watch the icy surge of water melt bulldoze its way through the boulder wreckage of the last ice-dam burst. I stood alone with no one to explain this sight to me, but too enthralled to want to dissect it with the dull blade of language.

I go into wilderness to bear the burden of too much beauty. I believe the urge to seek out beauty will be the salvation of a healthy planet. There is nothing like the exquisiteness and strength of the natural world—in size, in multiplicity, in amplification, in subtlety. It demands both attunement and atonement. Often as I drive along Saratoga Passage, or along the Pacific Ocean in a winter storm, or along Turnagain Arm, I wonder how it is that some appreciate the beauty in nature while others only its potential to profit a few.

I go out to record and research and celebrate those intricate loops of energy that are recycling through Nature's black box into more and more complex life forms. Mushrooms, for example, are fundamental to the forest's economy, nurturing and stabilizing the roots of new trees, releasing organic material from once-living plants into the soil as nutrients for future plants. Nothing is wasted in fungal activity. Everything dead is once again brought to life through the soil's mysteries.

Each woman goes out into the wilderness at a different level—from hanging from rock to rock by one's toes, to barreling down dangerous whitewater, to quietly studying an insect going about its curiously wonderful business. For so long, unfounded fears and cultural propriety have imprisoned us in static, man-made rooms. Not going out at all is not an option if we are to remain healthy. We can no longer afford to live by unfounded fears.

Our humanity and womanhood are grounded in and amplified by our contact with wilderness. Those of us who keep field journals, however elaborate or simple, have found that these notebooks start the dark alchemy in which fact, sweat, and fond memory ferment and develop into a psychic perfume to be applied for years and years.

Susan Zwinger, an activist, poet, lecturer, and writer on the environment and environmental issues, was given the Governor's Writers Award for her book, Stalking the Ice Dragon. *She lives in Langley, Washington. This piece was excerpted from her book,* Women in Wilderness, *which she co-edited with her mother, Ann Zwinger.*

★

While I covet rare time in the field spent alone, I also cherish the time spent with my marvelous daughter. She is a generous and articulate teacher. We share many outdoor memories and wilderness is the fabric onto which we embroider our experiences. Our relationship as mother and daughter and as friends has evolved from a wander across an Arkansas field when she was a little girl, to hours spent leaning over a tidal pool in Baja California, to long treks lugging backpacks through high altitude fell fields just months ago. We were camped at 10,500 feet near timberline, alongside a stream. On this trip, which included Susan's birthday, we raised a toast of freshly filtered, very cold stream water to the pleasures of wilderness and the vagaries that brought us there.

I inherited my wilderness genes from my daughter. It was she who first did wilderness camping, it was she who first went into the wilderness of Utah and came back beaming, it was she who drove alone to Alaska. From her experience and sturdy outlook I have taken courage and encouragement, both words from Middle English root meaning "heart." Susan brought me up from a very timorous housewife to a rabid seeker of solitude.

Susan's track is different from mine, for we are separated by a generation. "Ecology" was not in my vocabulary until college. "Environmentalism" didn't arrive until Earth Day, 1970. Susan grew up realizing that there were some knotty environmental dilemmas that her generation was going to have to solve. She does not waste time on blame but moves quickly and works hard to better conditions, especially those that are still salvageable. She has endured threats, something I've never had to do (my worst epithet is the little-old-lady-in-tennis-shoes curse and being negated because I'm a woman.) Because of Susan, I have a sharper view of the world today. She is an activist, poet, and artist, an indefatigable writer, and lecturer on such problem areas as old growth forests. Her words and thoughts are not mine, nor should they be, nor could they be, but in them I see my hopes and dreams and ideals.

—Ann Zwinger, "Natural Connections," *Women in Wilderness*

CLAIRE WALTER

✦ ✦ ✦

Coming of Age on Bali

The author reflects on an
ancient island ritual.

"WOULD YOU LIKE TO SEE A MENSTRUATION CEREMONY?"
The invitation was disconcerting. Intriguing, but disconcerting to one who grew up when such functions were rarely mentioned, let alone celebrated. Publicly celebrated. I'd heard that visitors are often invited to Balinese funerals, Balinese weddings, Balinese feasts. But something as personal as this? Since no funeral, wedding, or other feast seemed to present itself, I accepted.

That no other invitation was forthcoming was in itself surprising, Balinese celebrations are myriad. With the Indian Ocean to the west and the Pacific to the east, Bali is a Hindu island in a predominantly Muslim archipelago. Thinking of themselves as Balinese first and as Indonesians a distant second, the earthy people of this enchanted island enhance every aspect of life.

The first ceremony in Balinese Hinduism is three months after conception. The last is the cremation, which can be several years after a person has passed on—once the family has saved enough money to send the deceased off in suitable style. Ceremonies may take place in a village temple or in a family compound, which is why I was to witness the coming of age of a stranger in the home of a family I didn't know.

173

It's all a manifestation of a religion that is the epicenter both of individual Balinese lives and communal culture. This is not an ascetic Hinduism of meditation and denial. Rather, it is a rollicking religion which honors the gods in a myriad of joyous ways—architectural, decorative, musical, and especially ritual.

Decoration knows no bounds. Every surface of every important building is covered with rich, imaginative, and often lusty carvings. Ceremonial cloths of bright red, yellow, or checkered black and white adorn the anthropomorphic stone sculptures that appear everywhere. Small square baskets filled with flowers and fruit appear as daily offerings on village shrines, in front of places of business and even on the hoods of rental cars to assure good fortune.

Whether one of life's many ceremonies is held at home or in a temple, elaborately arranged offerings are made to the gods. Flags and banners flutter in the breeze. Fringed umbrellas and ornately embroidered cloth panels add even more color to an already bright scene. The air is sweet with incense and the heady music of the *gamelan*, a xylophone-like instrument that is the staple of Balinese music.

So there we sat, the other menstruation celebration guests and I, on folding chairs in the home of the girl whose new maturity we were honoring. My place was along a covered portico between the heavy front gate and the courtyard where the ceremony would take place.

The *gamelan* played without respite, and sarong-clad women bearing elaborate towers of fruit and flowers on their heads filed past on the way to the main altar around the corner in the courtyard's largest section. Men brought in tubs of meats and poultry, as well as a chicken for a ritual slaughter.

Then the guest of honor, clad in a golden sarong, was carried into the enclosure on the shoulders of two young men. She was accompanied by two pubescent boys, cousins I was told, who shared her day because they too were coming of age. The girl was a graceful beauty, who looked discretely proud. She wore a gold headdress of traditional design, but was lipsticked into modern womanhood—rather symbolic, I thought, of ancient Balinese traditions in conjunction with the late 20th century.

The boys, also riding on men's shoulders, seemed bored. One was toothpick-thin and appeared to verge on restlessness. The other, pudgy and sullen, kept looking toward the kitchen, from which drifted aromas of the banquet that would follow.

The procession wound to the altar where the ceremony took place. Older men and women, seated separately, had the best places—close, just before the altar. I could see them, but not the ceremony itself, and for a while I watched the old folks watching what was actually going on. Eventually, I found myself drifting off into a dreamy state, furthered by the heat of an early Balinese afternoon and the sensory overload of the colors and sounds and smells.

Through my haziness, an insight emerged, nothing cosmic, just one of those realizations of the obvious that nonetheless satisfies. A joyous celebration of a girl's very clear transition in life, shared by her male peers, no matter how reluctant or bored, seemed preferable to furtiveness, snickering, and the other traditional Western responses to coming of age—or many other of life's transitions. The Balinese do it better.

Claire Walter is an award-winning writer living in Boulder, Colorado, with her husband Ral Sandberg and her son Andrew Cameron-Walter. Her own "menstruation celebration" consisted of being allowed a day off from junior high school. She is Skiing *magazine's travel editor and the author of* The Complete Idiot's Guide to Skiing, Rocky Mountain Skiing, Skiing on a Budget, *and other books.*

＊

Walking home in a soft twilight, we hear the music, see the lights, slip under a tent where the women of the Bride's family are dancing to sitars and drums. They sweep us in, Jane and me, make us eat, drink, surround us, hover, ask our names. Now we are strewn with wreaths of marigolds; now they are touching our hair. We fall back in our chairs, dizzy with the overkill of satins, lamés, and silks in vibrating colors on the little girls, stunningly made up! Then the Mother of the Bride opens my palm and smacks me, hard, with a blop of something that I fear is cow dung, or worse, and makes me hold it tight—so the dye will take, I find out. I have been blessed with henna, the Good Luck tattoo of the Indian subcontinent.

—Virginia Barton Brownback, "Pakistan Passages"

$\star$ $\overset{\star}{}$ $\star$

The Magic Side of Time

Undertaking a South American odyssey
with a nine-year-old in tow.

FOR SIX MONTHS WE'D BEEN PLANNING TO TAKE THE SATURDAY
train from Puno, on the Peruvian shore of Lake Titicaca, across the
Altiplano, to the Inca city of Cuzco. But there we were, in Puno,
the night before the train was supposed to leave, and we still did-
n't have tickets. Not for a lack of effort. Gene and I, our nine-year-
old son, Gino, and our brother Mike had all trooped in to a travel
agency in Santiago, Chile, expressly to make train reservations. The
travel agent said we'd have to wait until we were actually in Peru.
In Arequipa a Peruvian travel agent said we could only get tickets
in Puno, where we were going to catch the train. She told us the
train wasn't running anyway because a bridge was out along the
route. In Puno we discovered that the only place to get tickets was
the train station. It was closed. The station would be open the next
morning before the 7:00 a.m. train to Cuzco. And so it went.

Gino says "Titicaca" more often than necessary. He's impressed
with the highest lake in the world, but he's even more intrigued
with its name. Only a child could take such delight in saying forbidden words without reprimand. He's sending his third grade class

in California a picture postcard of the lake. He knows his classmates will laugh. Titi...caca. Get it?

There's nothing lighthearted in the appearance of Lake Titicaca. She's a spectacular bottomless cerulean. She's serious and cold. She looks like she'd swallow up anyone who tried to do something as frivolous on her as jet skiing or drinking beer on a party boat.

We hired a boat and guide to take us to the floating reed islands of the Uro Indians. Our handbook suggested that instead of giving the Uro children money, we should give them fruit, paper, or pencils. Four oranges were all we had on hand, so that's what we took. When I saw how ravenous the children were, my motherly instincts made me want to rush back to the mainland for more fruit. Fresh fruit and vegetables are rare treats for them. They have no refrigeration, no stores, no orchards or gardens. There isn't any soil on which to farm. Although our feet didn't get wet walking on the island, we were as close to walking on water as we're ever likely to get. The reeds that make up the island aren't attached to the bottom of the deep lake.

> *R*olling back onto my stomach, I started swimming again. On this extreme swim across Lake Titicaca, I was going to have to make a choice: to breathe or maintain a core temperature. At that point, breathing seemed more important. So I cut my speed from two knots to one. Quickly the fifty-six degree water numbed my skin. But I was thankful for that.
>
> During my workouts in the lake I had gotten sunburned and something had been biting me. My body was covered with quarter-sized pink spots that itched worse than mosquito bites. No one, not even the doctors in La Paz, knew what organism was causing them. Few people ever swim in Lake Titicaca. Those who did wore wet suits.
>
> ◆
>
> —Lynne Cox,
> "Breathless in Bolivia," *Travelers' Tales: Women in the Wild*

Reeds are continuously being harvested and piled on top of the old ones to keep the islands afloat. The islanders' huts and boats are made of reeds, as are the toy boats they sell to tourists.

"Can I have a boat?" asked Gino. We got him two.

All the children had chapped, red cheeks. None of the little ones had any clothes from the waist down while we were glad to be wearing heavy wool sweaters. A child walked to the edge of the island and peed into the water.

"Don't they have bathrooms?" asked Gino.

"No," Gene said. "It's like backpacking."

"If I was on this camping trip, I'd want to go home," Gino said. "It's too cold and windy here."

"But they are home," I said.

"I feel sorry for them," Gino said.

Waking up the next morning at 5:00 a.m. for a train trip we might not get to take was tough, but we packed our bags, checked out of the hotel, and headed for the station as though four tickets were waiting for us. And they were. After our failed efforts to get tickets in advance for this famous train trip and after tales of bridges out and trains not running, it seemed incredible that we were doing exactly what we had planned for so long to be doing on this morning. Maybe we were on the magic side of time.

Gene chained our luggage to an overhead rack, and we settled into our seats on the side of the train where the best views would be. A table with two of us on one side, two on the other, added a good deal to the comfort of the eleven-hour trip. Most people can't look at scenery for eleven hours straight. Nine-year-old people certainly can't. Part of the time Gino and his dad played Yahtzee, a game Gino could carry in his little pocket: five dice with paper and a pencil for keeping score. The dice and a deck of cards were all we'd brought for him to play with during the two months we were in South America. We'd brought ten books for him, and he'd read them all before we were midway through our travels. It's difficult to find children's books in English in South America. Luckily, children don't mind reading the same book over and over.

Lunch was served to us on real plates at our table. While my mouth tasted juicy baked chicken and rice, my eyes feasted on glaciated mountain peaks, small groups of llamas, and Indian women in black bowler hats and multilayered skirts. Every time our red and yellow train made a stop, vendors rushed the windows on both sides of the cars selling drinks, fresh fruit, cooked corn on the cob, meat pies called *empanadas*, and various handicrafts including fluffy toy llamas in different sizes. One toothless old woman waved her little llamas in the open window by Gino.

"*No, gracias,*" he said.

Quickly, she pushed a larger stuffed animal through the window into his face. He leaned away from her and emphatically repeated, "*¡No gracias!*" The train started moving slowly. The old woman trotted along next to us, waving her wares until the train picked up speed and left her behind.

"I'm surprised you didn't want one," I said.

"She wasn't a very good salesperson," said Gino. "She just about punched me out with that big one."

Mike said, "If it weren't for her wad of coca leaves, she wouldn't have anything at all in her mouth."

"Does chewing coca leaves make your teeth fall out?" asked Gino.

Gene said, "She's probably just too poor to get proper dental care."

I resisted the motherly temptation to segue into a lecture on the importance of good oral hygiene and not eating too many sweets, but I couldn't resist giving a brief history lesson.

As we continued across the Altiplano, I told Gino, "We're following the path of the first Incas, Manco Capac and his wife, Mama Ocllo. According to Inca legend, they emerged from Lake Titicaca. After a time, they traveled to a beautiful valley where they established Cuzco and brought civilization to the world."

"I guess they didn't have trains then?" Gino asked.

Mike laughed. "Good one, Gino."

I wasn't sure Gino had meant to make a wisecrack. I thought he might be trying to get a perspective on what the world had been like back then.

"I'm glad they have trains now," he said, and cuddled up to me for a nap.

I wondered if Gino would remember this day for the rest of his life. I knew he'd cherish whatever memories he kept of this trip, as his father and I fondly recall the family vacations of our childhoods.

There are those who prefer to travel by themselves and speak of the lucidity of loneliness. Nobody will grumble that they've chosen a hotel that's too expensive or too shabby. They don't have to play Yahtzee or read children's books. They don't have to please anyone but themselves, but that means there's no one to help or entertain them either. I prefer the camaraderie and closeness of family travel. There's a synergy in sharing that gives a legendary quality to shared memories. Family travel provides an opportunity for parents and children, relatives and friends, to be together on the magic side of time.

Motherhood is the scariest, costliest, longest, and most rewarding trip Mary Gaffney has made. She and her husband and their three children live in the redwoods of Northern California. Her writing also appeared in Travelers' Tales Brazil *and* Travelers' Tales Love & Romance.

*

On a recent trip to Guatemala City the wonderful unbounded glories of a child's mind were delightfully brought home to me. As I waited in the lobby of a large bank building, I watched a young mother in country dress with her little boy, whom I guessed to be about five years old. "Stay here and wait for me," she directed as she disappeared into an office. As the child fidgeted he became fascinated by a door from which people emerged when a button was pushed. Tentatively he approached the closed door, pushed the button, and within seconds a smiling woman emerged. Another push elicited two businessmen. As he pushed the button again and again a steady flow of people continued to materialize. The child was entranced. "We have to leave now," called his mother when she returned. "Oh please, mama," he pleaded, "let me push the button again and make some more people." With a smile his mother waited for the elevator door to open one more time.

—Judy Wade, "The Magic of Childhood"

⋆ ＊ ⋆

Work It, Girlfriend

*A long-distance move brings a mother
and daughter closer together.*

"YOU'RE JUST HERE FOR THE MORAL SUPPORT," ASHLEY SAYS watching me. "I drove it last night from the rental place and I can do it alone."

I'm standing in the humid sunshine of an Ohio July morning staring at an enormous moving van and questioning my own judgment. When I have filled my eyes with the behemoth, I stare at the apple red BMW, my twenty-something daughter's delight that we'll be towing behind the moving van from Cincinnati to California. This all began when my daughter stated she was going to drive back to California by herself.

"You can't do that. It just isn't safe," I'd heard myself say. "I'll fly out and drive back with you."

"Only if you really want to, Mom," she'd said.

"I really want to," I'd said. "It'll be an adventure." I bought my plane ticket and worked on convincing myself that everything would be all right, reminding myself of how many times I'd seen just such combos rolling insouciantly along one or another of our nation's highways. I'd always wanted to write a road story and this would be material. I was getting stodgy and this would shake up my life. It would be a chance for us to spend some time together.

Inside, the van has air-conditioning, a radio, power steering, automatic transmission—everything, it seems, for people like us who've never gone to trucking school. We call a local garage and they send out a young man to help us put the car on the trailer. He tells us this is the first time he's ever done such a job. We watch him lash the car's tires on with flimsy-looking fabric straps. When he's done, the two chains that hook the car to the tow rig are dragging the ground. He seems to think this is okay and since we don't know better, we leave it that way.

A man from the apartments comes out and notices that the screw that holds the trailer onto the ball on the truck isn't on all the way. He screws it down more. None of this seems very auspicious. We check the cargo inside the truck and tie things down. Ashley puts her house plants on the front seat of the Beemer so they'll get light as we drive.

With great panache, Ashley drives away from the apartment complex where she's lived since her divorce and onto the freeway. Each time an eighteen-wheeler passes, our van shudders, sucked toward the larger vehicle. Some sort or vacuum effect I think, watching Ashley grimace, her jaw set, and her knuckles white as they grip the steering wheel.

"You're doing great," I say as we turn onto a cloverleaf. I look back to see the Beemer following rump up, nose down like a dog on a scent being pulled backwards. We high five and chortle.

"Work it, girlfriend," Ashley says.

We enter Indiana. Lush fields of corn, farmhouses, barns flow by, rivers spill over their banks. This is the wettest summer on record in the Midwest and cumulus clouds edge up the horizon.

Our first road test comes when I have to pee. Ashley turns wide and glides smoothly under a gas station awning—backing is impossible with the tow rig. I run in and use the bathroom. In the truck again I see a big red notice on the dashboard. WARNING: 11' 0" CLEARANCE. MOST TRUCK RENTAL ACCIDENTS RESULT FROM DRIVING UNDER LOW BRIDGES, SERVICE STATION CANOPIES, ETC.

"Did you think about clearance?" I ask. She shakes her head.

Our next test comes when we need fuel. We're talking fuel, not gas. Diesel. In the glove compartment we find an extensive manual on the sound system but only a tiny brochure on the truck and no information on a fuel tank. We walk around the truck realizing we're being watched by the "real" truckers. Finally we decide that the ugly black drum hidden under the box of the truck must be it. A screw top with a sign saying DIESEL FUEL ONLY confirms this. As Ashley squats with the hose on the glowing asphalt, I clean the windshield.

"The one thing the rental people stressed was checking the oil," Ashley says when we're done. Fine. We've both put oil in cars. We walk to the front of the truck ready to lift the hood and discover there is no hood. In fact, judging from the flat front of the truck there doesn't seem to be any engine. We check the brochure again but there's nothing on this situation either. Still, we know there has to be an engine because something did make noise when she turned the key. We locate a diagram inside the driver's door showing that an engine does exist—right under the seat. To get to it we'd have to lift the whole cab of the truck which seems a little extreme just to put in a quart of oil. Finally, between the cab and the box, I discover a small plastic cup with a cap that says CHECK OIL HERE. Next to it is a dipstick. We check the oil and it seems to be down, very down.

Of course, we get not a clue from the brochure about what sort of oil to put in. A trucker and his son, who's about Ashley's age and who seems to think Ashley in her pink shorts and baggy t-shirt with her Pebbles Flintstone ponytail is pretty cute, are happy to show us what kind of oil they buy. We buy a gallon and fill the plastic cup, wondering if this is indeed the right place to put the oil.

Back on the road we hear an ominous growling sound right behind us, where we put the oil. At the next exit we call the 800 number also pasted on the dashboard. Someone on the other end who doesn't speak much English says not to worry.

"Work it, girlfriend," we say as we plunge into Illinois, through Peoria, then through Galesburg, home of Carl Sandburg. Dusk arrives and I insist that we stop at the next motel so that we can cross the Mississippi River in full daylight to best gaze upon the

vastness of its new surface. We talk about relaxing in a motel with
a glass of wine. We talk about a party. "Toga. Toga. Toga," we
chant. We're getting giddy. The road gets worse. I can feel Ashley
getting tired. We drive past signs saying Rock Island, Moline,
Chicago, names from Bob Seger songs. No motels appear. A brilliant sunset flares and we try to appreciate it while watching fireflies glittering in the grass. Then we hit a huge hole and another
truck tries to run us down.

Suddenly we're on Interstate 80 and crossing the bridge to
Iowa. Only inches below the Mississippi stretches—an ocean, its
pewter surface streaked by moonlight and broken by the tops of
trees, the roofs of houses.

As we turn into Davenport nothing looks awash. The motel
manager scowls when I mention floods and says, "That's just a few
streets down by the river." We walk out into the humid night and
buy wine coolers and popcorn and come back to the big cold
room to watch Jay Leno and take turns in the shower.

Iowa, which is widely supposed to be under water, is only
flooded in the logical places. The rest looks green and lovely. The
road narrows to one lane each way as road crews make repairs. It
rains. By mid-morning Ashley is frazzled and I suggest a stop. As if
by magic, a gleaming white city appears on a hilltop in the middle
of a huge corn field. We pull into the biggest outlet mall ever.
Everyone in Iowa who is not bailing is here. We check out what
Ralph Lauren, Reebok, and Liz Claiborne have to offer but our
only purchases are a couple of Arby's chicken sandwiches.

Near Des Moines we finally see some flooding in low areas. We
have a Diet Coke at Burger King because they have the easiest
parking lot to get in to and out of. Because of our size we park
with the truckers. More rain. We see a sign pointing to Sioux City.
"Where all the lawyers live," says Ashley. By late afternoon we cross
the Missouri River and enter Nebraska. It's pouring when we hit
Lincoln and find a motel only to discover everything's full because
a Jehovah's Witness convention is in town. We are so daunted, the
desk clerk takes pity and scours us a room in a place across town.

The next morning I announce I am going to drive. Ashley tells me I don't have to, but I can tell that it's time. The rain lets up. We pass a sign directing us to Buffalo Bill's house. This is Willa Cather country. I remember reading *O Pioneers!* in college and being overwhelmed by the grimness of prairie life. We are now paralleling the Oregon Trail. Wind blows the alders along the North Platte River.

I begin driving. Not bad, I think at first, then *whoa*. The Beemer is really fishtailing behind us. I wonder if it's shifted on its trailer. I pull into a service station at the next off ramp and a nice me-

Age is something that doesn't matter unless you are a cheese.

—Actress Billie Burke, aka Glenda the Good Witch in *The Wizard of Oz*

chanic—everyone is nice in the Midwest—says the Beemer is okay but the straps are loose and the safety chains left dragging are ground all the way through.

We call the rental people and talk this time to a Cajun in Lafayette, Louisiana, who directs us back 26 miles to a town where the chains can be welded. We take a side road and get right up close to all that corn, passing old houses, silos, all quiet except for insect noises. Red-winged blackbirds and a prairie falcon pattern the air. We arrive at a big barn full of farm vehicles being repaired by a sooty-faced welder. Here we find out that the safety chains securing the tow rig to the truck weren't secured correctly. For the first time in years I think about my guardian angel and say a prayer of thanks.

By dusk we've made it to Ogalala and the 100th meridian. The air is dry. Even the breeze feels western. We drink wine in the lounge of the motel, a '50s style room with a huge television, and four or five ranchers, compact sun-tanned men in jeans and checkered shirts, at the bar. Ashley and I talk and watch *Seinfeld* on the giant television. The evening takes on a lighter cast as tensions slip away. I call home and report our progress.

At a truck stop the next morning, we fill up surrounded by shirtless, tattooed young men, the kind Brad Pitt must have studied before he tried out for the part in *Thelma and Louise*. Ashley tells me to lock the doors and stay inside while she fills the tank and cleans the windshield. I should be telling her that. She's the one they're eyeing. She's awfully protective of me, which I find very touching. As she goes in to pay, a commotion breaks out among several men huddled together and I hear shouting. My heart pounds. The huddle breaks up and the men are laughing. My heart is still pounding when I see Ashley come out.

Sunflowers line the side roads, windmills, wheat fields—no more corn. The land seems to swell. When you're on the top of a hill and you look out you see not the horizon but the land dropping away. "The sky just takes over," says Ashley.

We drive through Cheyenne, a cluster of buildings around the gilded dome of the capitol. The air smells of gas. Houses are scarcer here and trailers litter the landscape as haphazardly as if dropped from the sky. The Laramie valley is flecked with clouds. After Laramie, the rain begins and the wind comes up. The road turns nasty and rutted and the Beemer fishtails madly. Ashley grits her teeth. At Rawlins I take over. The road improves a little, but fighting the wind and the road is tiring. At a stop on Elk Mountain, where gray clouds threaten snow, a young man tells us its been like this all summer. Mines and oil fields pass by.

The next day we climb into the Wasatch Mountains with their lush valleys and pass through Park City, a jarring display of condos spilling down around yet another outlet mall. The descent to Salt Lake City is steep and terrifying and I smell our brakes all the way down. We zip through Salt Lake City and the salt flats so white they might be snow.

Over Nevada the wind forms a glass shelf with fat saucy clouds sitting on it. Trails of snow linger in the crevices of mountains. We're tasting home now driving through sage and creosote bush and pine and cedar. There's almost no traffic today and the driving is relatively easy. Ashley talks about doing outdoor things back in California. She wants a wind-surfer, a pick-up truck.

We stop for the night in Lovelock and drink margaritas at a bar whose surface contains video screens. Ashley speculates on the nature of gamblers. "They're optimists," she says. "They believe they'll win."

"Maybe so," I say, "but the idea of trusting in blind luck doesn't appeal to me." We watch an old couple sitting in front of a bank of machines, the woman feeding coins, the man studying a board overhead flashing numbers. His face is rapt.

We can almost smell the Pacific by now. Leaving Reno we cheer at the "ENTERING CALIFORNIA" sign as we climb the impossibly beautiful granite Sierras. The decline into the Sacramento Valley is hairy. From Auburn on, cars pour in from every entrance, everyone moving full throttle. We can feel the tension. I almost long for those empty Nevada highways. If I didn't know that my little home in Sonoma County was waiting, I might be tempted to turn around.

Finally we pull off onto a two lane road and a bucolic landscape of vineyards alternating with forest and the occasional dairy herd unfolds. Napa. Sonoma. Penngrove. Cotati. Highway 116 appears like the yellow brick road and our destination, Sebastopol, is the Emerald City. "Work it, girlfriend," we say and high five as we pull over for the last time.

Four months later I'll get a call at four a.m. telling me my mother has died. I must cross the country once more. I call Ashley. "I need you to come with me to Louisiana," I tell her. "Moral support."

Robin Beeman lives in Occidental, California and has published two books, A Parallel Life and Other Stories *and* A Minus Tide. *This story first appeared in* Cartwheels on the Faultline.

✶

Only a day or two into our travels, I was forced to conclude that a major reversal had taken place: I was now the mother, and she, Helene, the child. As I wrote in my journal at the time: "Mother and I are definitely driving each other to...new areas of understanding!" I was surprised at her naiveté and fearfullness, and recognized that she was really having to push herself. With travel, of course, comes the constant bombardment of the new, the searching out of comfort, familiarity, relativity. I was going through it as much as she was, so how was I to respond when she'd ask me, for the *n*th time: "What's that?" or "Why are they doing that?" My inevitable answer: *"I don't know!!"*

—Terri Hinte, "The Bohemians"

LAURA CUNNINGHAM

* * *

Mother in a Strange Land

In Romania, a woman seeks clues to the mysteries
of her adopted baby's life.

COULD THERE BE A JOURNEY MORE FATEFUL THAN THE OVERSEAS odyssey to adopt a foreign child? The United States immigration service refers to these prospective new citizens in the preliminary papers as "unidentified orphans," and, after their arrival in this country, as "resident aliens." In the 1990s, what I think of as an adoption excursion has become a more common, and surreal, experience. Every day, hopeful adoptive parents fly off to Asia, Eastern Europe, and Latin America on journeys that will forever change their lives. I have taken two such journeys, the first to Romania, the second to China. But that first trip was my introduction to the depth of revelation that such a trip entails.

It was several years ago that I traveled to Transylvania to adopt an infant girl. While initially I was startled by the sightseeing aspects—interpreters and guides will insist you visit the local attractions—I came to value these experiences. When might I ever see my baby's native land again? Would I ever view a country and a culture with more curiosity? I carry with me not just photographs and videotapes, but clues to the mysteries of my child's life.

My trip to Romania had an ominous start: my husband and I arrived in the aftermath of the bloody 1989 revolution. All I knew of the country was the news footage of slain student revolutionaries, and the crumpled bodies of the fallen dictator, Nicolae Ceausescu, and his wife. We were accompanied by a Romanian friend, who would serve as our interpreter and guide; she told tales of fleeing Romania's oppression and appeared uneasy about what we would find.

Not only that. A woman met me at Kennedy International Airport, on her return trip from Bucharest, and reported that she "hated Romania," that it was "awful—they have no lawns." This woman represented, I discovered later, if not the Ugly American version of an adoptive parent, at least a sort of Homely American. Later I met several people who sought out Cokes and hamburgers in Bucharest. But I also met many more adoptive parents who in a sense "adopted" their child's native country. All the adoptive parents reported a time-machine sense of dislocation: one day, you find yourself not only holding a newborn baby but standing in the shadow of Dracula's castle as well.

The time shock was instantaneous. Walking into our Bucharest hotel room, I entered history: the walls were pocked with bullet holes; the window was cracked. Through shattered glass, I saw the rusted armature of the burned-out television station that had been the focus of much of the fighting. I concentrated on every detail in order to tell my daughter someday, for her history was related to this carnage. She was the "unidentified orphan" of the firestorm—not an orphan in the sense of having lost two parents to death, but by decree. Ceausescu had outlawed all contraception and abortion. As a result, there were at that time thousands of unwanted babies and children left in orphanages and hospitals. On my first walk through the city, I saw its morbid center, the plaza marked by dying bouquets, where the students had been killed. I took my first mental snapshots of the wilted flowers and charred tapers, the black stain that shadowed the city.

Almost immediately, we boarded a train bound for the Carpathian Mountains, where "our" baby had been born, and where she waited, in a hospital, in a tiny mountain village. The trip took perhaps three hours, but it transported me, it seemed, three centuries into Romania's past. The passenger cars were barely lighted—electricity being rationed—and there had been little plumbing repair in the past several years. The air was thick with the smoke of Carpati cigarettes, redolent of the Turkish influence that I would observe throughout this section of Romania. The train windows, cataracted with grime, still offered a view of beautiful countryside. Beside the track, a river ran quick and silver; gorges plunged.

At nightfall, we arrived at the station in Brasov. The dimness prevailed here, too, turning the main room into a cathedral of shadow from which vendors loomed, offering hot crepes. Because we could not meet the baby's doctor until dawn, my husband, our friend the translator, and I took a taxi to a small stone house on the mountainside, the summer home of the interpreter's grandparents. The house had no plumbing, but featured pretty porcelain stoves set in the corners of the rooms. The beds seemed ancient; their covers, shaken, gave off plumes of dust. I spent a sleepless night, staring out at the Carpathian sky, studded with stars brighter than I'd ever seen.

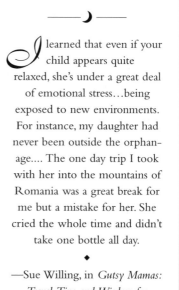

I learned that even if your child appears quite relaxed, she's under a great deal of emotional stress...being exposed to new environments. For instance, my daughter had never been outside the orphanage.... The one day trip I took with her into the mountains of Romania was a great break for me but a mistake for her. She cried the whole time and didn't take one bottle all day.

◆

—Sue Willing, in *Gutsy Mamas: Travel Tips and Wisdom for Mothers on the Road,* by Marybeth Bond

At dawn I saw just how pristine the Carpathian villages had remained. More traffic was horse-drawn than motorized. The streets were cobbled; the village lanes, steep. People and animals seemed to walk at a tilt. We drove through a pastoral landscape such as I had seen only in the works of Old Masters. Here was agriculture unchanged since the 1500s. Horses drew the plows. Cowherds milked, by hand, in the fields. Everywhere, shepherds and goatherds led their flocks. We stopped often on the narrow roads to let the men and their animals pass. What struck me, then, was the sweet silence—how quiet the past had been, how still, before the advent of the engine.

As if in compensation, the pediatrician drove, Romanian-style, full-speed, roaring around the hairpin turns, despite the sight, all too frequent, of charred cars along the road. I was startled to see large signs with the image of a fanged and roaring bear, warning of the presence of these beasts. The Romanian bears, I learned, were not the shuffling beggars at home, but giant, man-eating brown bears. The doctor told me my prospective baby's family had for generations patrolled these woods as gamekeepers. I stared out at the primeval shadows: this was my daughter's history, and I vowed to respect it. Soon the Transylvanian forests gave way to pastures dotted with sheep. A mist draped the valley and, as we drove toward the rising sun, I felt we'd ripped through the curtain of fog, like scrim, to enter the light of the new day.

There, in a tiny town—in a square, cement hospital—my future waited. The hospital too, seemed from another century, not in its interior, but in the formality and style of its occupants. Inside, the nurses wore formal uniforms that seemed to date back a few decades. Women who were patients clustered in a lobby, wearing *babushkas* and skirt-and-blouse ensembles that showed a daring chic in their clashing colors and pattern. Some suckled babies. Walking past, I trembled. How dare I trespass into this world and presume to be the mother of a baby born here? I know I was crossing more than one border.

I hurried up the stairs, my heart hammering. In the doctor's office—a surprise. A nurse had peeked from the window and counted the exact number of our party, and now waited, proffering a linen-draped tray holding demitasses of strong Turkish coffee. This was the gracious touch I needed to face the most dramatic moment of my life. I waited to meet my daughter. She was carried in, howling, her face framed by what appeared to be a

19th-century gauze bonnet. *Yowl!* She seemed to squawl. *Here I am.* Everyone smiled. She had a full head of thick black hair, and wide brown eyes that seemed to regard me with full recognition.

That night, the grown-ups celebrated with Romanian home-brew, the fiery *tuica*, which we tossed back in tiny shot glasses, with the local toast: *"Noroc!"* ("Good luck!") Our luck held through ribbons of red tape—baby visa, baby passport, baby medical tests. Then, after five weeks, we were winging our way back to the United States. I propped my new daughter up in her airline-approved baby seat and began the pragmatic part of being a mother. I changed my first diaper when we deplaned in Luxembourg. We reboarded—fresh diaper in place, warm formula on hand—and flew home across the night ocean.

Laura Cunningham is the author of Sleeping Arrangements.

*

Amy placed Danny in my arms. As I nuzzled the baby, she crowed over him like any proud mother. "Isn't he beautiful?" she said. "See how big he is? See? He knows it's you. He smiled."

I was lost in him. The bonds radiated from him and locked me fast. What could I say? How could I compliment her on the fine son she had borne? Facing me was the mother who had suffered a massive physical assault to give him life. A woman who had turned her back on her family's offers of help and her obstetrician's referral to a wealthy North Shore couple who could give this boy things we never could. Amy had not broken our trust. I appreciated that then. I'm awestruck by it now.

Amy and I traded Danny back and forth. Then his new father held him. "Oh, thank you," Dan said over and over. "Thank you. Thank you." It sounded like a prayer.

After a long time, a nurse poked her head in the room. "No one but the Mom is supposed to hold the baby," she said gently.

"But I—" I began, and stopped. Amy and I exchanged glances. I returned the baby to his bed. Amy covered him with a doll-size quilt. And then, straightening her shoulders, she began loading my arms with formula and diapers and little plastic containers of powder—all the free gifts that suppliers offer to maternity patients.

"I won't need these," she said firmly. "*You* will."

"I can't tell you..." I said.

Amy stopped me gracefully. "It's okay. I know."

—Jacquelyn Mitchard, "Mother to Mother," *The Adoption Reader:*
Birth Mothers, Adoptive Mothers and Adopted Daughters
Tell Their Stories, edited by Susan Wadia-Ells

TRICIA PEARSALL

* * *

Altitude Adjustment

The author contemplates the empty nest.

HUMMINGBIRDS WAKE UP BEFORE COWS. MOTHER NATURE IS definitely in control. There is no sadness in solitude. Powdered-eggs-and-jerky omelet is yummy. Lightning does whatever it wants to. Yellow-bellied marmots are downright nosy. A man sitting in a saddle is cockier than when standing on the ground.

"Got a gun?"

"You got guts, lady."

"Cute haircut!"

"Oh, God be with you."

"I wouldn't let no wife nor daughter of mine out on this trail alone! "

Just a few of the salvos I receive as I trudge the steep ascent entering the boulder-strewn, almost cartoon-gardened canyon formed by Williams Creek. Looks like the solo backpacking wilderness trip is becoming an annual event. Last year it was just me for eight days in the Glacier Peak Wilderness of Washington's Cascade Range. Then, it was more the challenge, "I can do it, by myself, and this is how!" This year, well, like Thoreau said, "I went to the woods because I wished to live deliberately, to confront only the essential facts of life, and see if I could not learn what it had to teach, and not, when I come to die, discover that I had not lived"—or dreamed to live! Well, that's a piece of this insatiable desire to hit the trail, and another part is to escape into the strenuous regimen and overwhelming beauty of the lonely, high western wilderness, to transfer my ruminating and digesting space from inside a dwelling to totally out of shelter.

My desire to go is also fueled by the impulsive ache to smell alpine meadows, to climb above treeline and dance among the peaks, to see original beauty and to be affronted by credible danger—the kind that Mother Nature dishes out, not that of some "in-your-face kid" whose attitude and anger are assuaged by his very own personalized assault weapon. I live in the city, smack dab in the middle of the city. For many summers, my husband and I and two hesitant, but polite, passive and probably bribed male children spent annual vacations backpacking in western wildernesses. In fact, we started the kids packing in the mountains of Virginia before they were six weeks old. When I broached the idea of a family excursion this year, I received solid encouragement and support for my solo expedition. More and more we all seem to madly pursue diverging paths, intensely delving into self-interests, be they rock concerts, rock climbing, memorizing television cartoons, or creating twentieth century showers out of nineteenth century plumbing. My divergence, alone to the mountains, I label an altitude adjustment, chucking impossible schedules and increasingly demanding financial obligations, fleeing the inanities of daily media feed, stopping to shake out the fuzzies, separating the essentials from the ever-surfacing, ever-present and well-spun chaff. It's reflecting on the friend who died of breast cancer in the spring and fear for the five more who were recently diagnosed. It's regaining humor about disjointed but perhaps well-intentioned families.

It's getting acclimatized to being a half-pasture or out-to-pasture mom, adjusting to what life will be after my sons soon take off. Ever since I was sent the mother-gift, the one moms receive when we first hear the wail of our offspring, that "ton of bricks" of unfathomed responsibility and commitment to nurture, my sons have occupied my last thought at bedtime and the first in the morning. It's a frightening feeling, this mother-gift. I will mourn the absence of my sons' physical presence, celebrate their independence and adventures and get over it and on with it, but it'll take a little adjustment, maybe more than one altitude adjustment. And now they flash to the world on their own, away to life.

The intensity of the act of going alone, of having all the colors of a field of high mountain flowers pierce my eyes alone, of being the only ears recording the pica squeals and moving boulders, means conversations are remembered; nothing is diffused in the melee of companionship. I am the sole receiver of and contributor to the experience and each instance must be remembered and logged. Space, outdoor space, allows this without any burden of guilt and for me, the need for space, slow motion and consideration far outweighs the immediate need for sharing experience or the often lonely exhaustion of such an endeavor. It's about quietude, solace, not miles hiked or mountains climbed. The Continental Divide mountains are the luxury vehicle.

I did actually extend a few overtures for companionship, only to be rebuffed by more enticing offers such as bell-choir rehearsal, trips to Omaha, practicing law, camp, fear, illness—any excuse. Opportunity doesn't knock often for an older-than-baby-boomer. Opportunities are created. I can't wait. Who knows? Next year I may need body part replacements. New multi-lens glasses grace my nose, and my mood swings are like bungee jumping off the New River Gorge Bridge. Some folks might suggest I go with a group, but I find the wilderness experience a very personal one, not easily shared with adult strangers. I don't relish inventing polite, stilted idle chatter or having some superior woodswomen eyeing my mistakes or intruding on an operatic impulse.

The trail begins at the end of a fifty-mile grass plain in the Weminuche Wilderness in southern Colorado, near the border of New Mexico. Much of this grass plain was inhabited by herds of sheep and cattle, but most of the used-to-be ranches are now developments fueled by Californians and Texans who have more money than taste. Imagine a huge, maybe twenty-thousand-square-foot, baby-blue Victorian wanna-be going up in the middle of a vast, flat plain. Not a tree in sight. Just other giant, neon, house-trees, future forests of America!

Climbing steeply in fits and starts, the ascent is broken by plateaus of lush meadows and stream crossings still following the creek valley. At around ten thousand feet I break into an amphitheater of aspens, at last above the dry ponderosa forest, the kind of tinder that is currently helping to spread a devastating fire forty miles to the east. Aspen trees are one of the signature pleasures of these Continental Divide mountains. A light wind moves their stiff, silvery-green leaves, releasing the sensual sounds of a syncopated rain stick. In certain special places, the bark of aspen trees is a guest register for the many mountain travelers who have passed by their trunks. Aspen art is a "log" revealing the names and dates of nineteenth century miners and sheep herders, as well as the flurry of backpackers from the 1960s to the present. On these particular trees, I can make out a few dates and initials higher up the trunks from the 1950s, maybe the 1940s, but most of the graffiti-like inscriptions date from the 1970s and 1980s. God, my vision is the pits, though; part of this half-century transition thing. These new lens-wonders do provide clarity at a distance, but I still want to push open a window to see the real world.

I am dehydrated and exhausted and have only hiked a few miles. It's the altitude, and once again, I am not in shape. Of course, this could be blamed on having arrived only yesterday from the humid, sea-level East Coast, but my body looks like a gravity experiment gone amuck, even though I run about four miles every other day. To combat dehydration I must drink at least three to four quarts of treated liquid per day. This results in having to extricate my warm, tired body from the deep folds of Moby Grape, my purple sleeping bag, to pee in the middle of the night. As I squat over carefully scooped earth, I look up to the most spectacular sky I have ever seen, galaxies beyond the Milky Way; not one inch of unused dark sky.

Last night, I logged twelve-and-a-half hours of much needed sleep, only waking when a few small fragments of these volcanic mountains came tumbling down to a lower resting place. Ah, gravity and shifting earth. I also heard a large tree snap in the dry wind. Today's climb is putting me up near the treeline. I seem to be experiencing a greater energy loss than anticipated, probably due to a slight infection, which has accompanied me from home. My pack weight, though, seems amazingly well-distributed and not unreasonable. Thank you, modern technology, for these newfangled energy bars. They certainly aren't on any gourmet menu, but they do work. The only pangs of loneliness come when I discover small rubber animals, home tokens, placed by family members within little crevices throughout my pack. It's mostly the beauty of the high alpine blooms and views that feel partially lost for not being shared.

Have only encountered five people so far and two were forest service personnel scouting campsites. No fire is allowed for any reason during this dry stretch. I finally reach what I think is a perfect spot high over a snow-fed creek looking into a glacial cirque on the Continental Divide. I am very tired and only realize the next day that the perfect spot has often been occupied by irreverent horse packers, evidenced by spent ropes, tackle, sardine cans, human waste, toilet paper and elk parts left behind. There is absolutely no reason for this abuse or careless abandon of an otherwise idyllic location. Given the opportunity, man will upset any precarious balance.

A wind shift in the mid-afternoon brings a strong, frosty breeze, forecasting the regular cycle of July thunderstorms. After a night of chills, fever and a horrid headache, I decide to lay over a day and count hummingbirds. Somebody left the sun in the closet, anyway. Sitting in a meadow below the tips of Indian paintbrush, nestled under thousands of white, yellow, blue, purple and orange wildflowers, I have the perfect vantage point for watching these crazy birds chase each other in a game resembling a frenetic *ménage à trois.* The entire meadow whirs; there are thousands, well, maybe hundreds, of these small, hyper, flying machines. When I look straight up, the clouds move in two separate directions. Amazing. The pleasure of this "lay-about" day is complemented by the Christmas aroma of spruce and fir, and the discovery of a tall waterfall with bathing pool, a ptarmigan or grouse family, a wheezing deer and a few invasive gray jays and Albert squirrels. And the greatest antidote to any less-than-energized day is food. Tonight, nut curry over couscous.

This crystal clear, blue-sky morning I am headed up to the Continental Divide Trail and south. Grits, cheese and salsa! A swim in the creek and up we go! This is why I keep backpacking. Inhaling this pleasure of the high mountains is spiritual armor for the return to family and urban inanities. A moment to revel, not to share. This is why I go alone. The climb out of the trees, out of the glacial cirques, along the snow-melt, boggy lakes, through the low ground cover growing on these gravelly peaks. This is the top of the world, the summit, where the water running west empties into the Pacific Ocean and east to the Atlantic Ocean—well, sort of. The view down into the valley on the other side, to which there is no trail, reveals two large herds of grazing elk. This is the ultimate brain Drano.

On the crest, following age-old cairns, a lone horseman passes with a train of four horses, a dog and rifle at his side.

"Where you headed?" I ask.

"Till it rains."

Looking up, a massive collection of dark, mean clouds are gathering over the northern peaks. I climb higher along the ridge and observe another storm mass to the south playing around the eastern valleys. Hey, it's only eleven in the morning. Don't sandwich me between these two weather beasts. On foot, I am keeping pace with the horseman, his plodding gait an imposed beacon, a mirage to follow. I'm hiking too fast.

I start yelling at the storms. "Screw off! Go away! Leave me alone!" I allow the horseman to fade into the mountain and climb around a mini-knife edge, a very precipitous peak. In front of me are huge cirques carved by fairly recent glaciers, snow ledges and the instantly recognized phenomenon of monadnocks, graphically illustrating dry geological texts. Amazing rock upthrusts and valleys. It's too much to digest.

Every time I stop to wallow in the vista, focus the camera or rearrange the pack, lightning and thunder kick me in the seat of the pants. Get moving! As I head down into a small valley punctuated by two glacial lakes, the huge rock faces behind me seem to have just been vomited from the earth, on fire, full of iron, sulfur and other seductive minerals. I walk out over a precipice to view a sheer drop to the thirty-mile valley below. I want to stop, savor, understand. Spit! Boom! Holy s——! Close, so close! *"Stay off ridges, out of caves and away from open meadows! Find shelter among dense, small trees in low areas."*

Across the snow fields; down the precipice; running, I finally reach a line of small bushes. Pass a lake and views, but no protection at all. The storms are closing fast, and I am running faster. My family would never believe this. Slow Mom, running with boots and pack, down steep rocks and gullies and not losing it, but scared stupid! Finally a lone tree, a lightning rod. Lightning like crazy! I feel a tingling sensation in my elbows. Now, three trees. Oh, where is the group of trees considered safe? It's raining, blowing, lightning. I see it exit the dark clouds. Hit the ground. Not far away. Then much closer. Finally, more trees. A group of midget trees in a field of larger ones, and I slide into home plate, huddling for an hour or more. Every time I raise my head, I see another long snake of orange fire seeking earth between the trees.

The night is white as the full moon rises between the downsloping arms of the fir trees. What if all these trees were tall buildings? Does an urban backpacker see the moon with the same fixation when it plays hide-and-seek with city rooftops?

I wake up the morning with that dreaded, all-too-familiar feminine feeling, the feeling that my entire inner body is being shed in the form of heavy bulbous clots of menstrual blood. Grabbing every piece of cloth I can find within easy reach, I stuff them between my legs and make a mad dash out of my sleeping bag, out of my bivy sack, and run barefoot for the environmentally-correct hole. At least get it in the right place, lest every bear within a fifty mile radius smells the scent. I've read that the scent of a woman menstruating attracts bears, and I believe most anything I read about bears, and about snakes and about crabs, for that matter. Course if a bear did smell my scent, it would probably detect an end-of-the-line menstruating female and go on picking berries. My sleep had been seasoned with cramping, but I thought I was dreaming. After all, it has only been two weeks since the last onslaught. Well, here I am, at almost eleven thousand feet, discharging heavy menses with only three Bounty Paper Towels—Select-Size.

In an effort to pair down bulk and weight in my backpack, I neglected to include "feminine protection." Well, who'd a' thought? Oh, how I just love this transition to the "golden years"—sex without worry, to estrogen or not to estrogen, calcium, oh calcium. I've been in female denial since I was thirteen, anyway, and I am only months from fifty. I still hate/resent the uncertainty and power of the female organs, that part of my body I do not commune with easily. Another hammer on the nail into feminine endurance. Imagine men putting up with this shit. I am well-prepared for all phases of this expedition, except for this, for which I am woefully unprepared, angry and frustrated.

All day, I hike down out of the mountains, to a grassy plateau. Miles of grassland extend beyond to a large lake. Somewhere near the lake, cattle are grazing. From the sound of it, one must be a bull. As I fall asleep, I watch the sun expose the over-twelve-thousand-foot peak above my head, giving a turquoise backdrop to the sky behind delicate orange clouds. They part to expose the planets, the galaxies of the setting sky lost to a full moon rise.

I don't know myself very well. I need fifty more years. This trip, it's just rain in the desert, fast, furious, intense, over shortly and barely enough to dampen the roots—but it's all there is until next season, all over for this year. Back to urban dangers, back to routine, back to the urban kitchen, back to solo urban ventures.

He wants to go around the corner, out, for supper? I don't mind cooking at all, in fact I'd rather. We can't afford to go out, anyway. He begs me to suit myself and saunters into the air-conditioned front room, taking his vodka tonic and newspapers with him.

I hurry back to the hot kitchen with relief. Reaching for the wooden cutting board, I begin to pare the garlic and onions into tiny cubes, the basic elements of the additive, the more-than-staple stew that will turn the beans, the soaked black beans, into a desirable, delectable, almost superlative offering for just another daily supper. Onion essence wafts upward to my nose and eyes. I am shedding tears, sobbing, at last allowed, without rebuke or even slight humiliation, to wash out the emotions of the day. This has been not just another roller-coaster day of fractured focus, but my son's graduation day, filled with a special blend of raging pride in my chid's coming of age and achievements never dreamed or expected. Choking in view of others would be confirmation of assumed weakness. It is easier to be robbed of such earned emotions.

The rhythm of dicing the green chilies soothes the difficult, exhausting realization that the roll of nurturer, of stimulant, of stalwart has terminated with the maturity revealed in the child today. Gently swirling the onions, garlic and chilies in the olive oil, the expanding odors of the heated cumin and cilantro signal the move toward a wakening inside me that must be seized lest I become a library of written moments. I pick up the wooden spoon to toss pork into the mixture and turn to see a silver wolf sitting inside the back door, brought by the currents of a past so extraordinary as not to accept a future of less.

I bend down to pick up the corn, to strip its sheath to its kernels while the wolf comes to rest the fur of its full torso next to my legs. The warmth of its strength gives me comfort in expelling the tears of realization, in adjusting to an empty change. I smile, accepting the tranquil pace of shucking each naked ear of corn, which I place in a large pot of water on the stove.

As I quarter small tomatoes, I am overcome with a sense of good fortune to encounter this silver wolf, to inhale yet again the fields, streams and woodlands from whence it has come. Mixing the tomatoes with the meat, I let the stew simmer while the rice steams. The wolf paces in circles at the foot of the stove, brushing the hem of my dress at each turn. I lean over to turn down the heat under the corn. As I walk away to fetch the dinner plates, the wolf leaps toward me, readjusting his path as he escapes through the open window, through the billowing gauze curtains. I smile calmly, serenely, reaching up to retrieve the china.

Tricia Pearsall has worked for the Historic Richmond Foundation and is currently a Director for St. Catherine's School. She would rather be backpacking with her family or alone in the high mountains. This story appeared in Solo: On Her Own Adventure, *edited by Susan Fox Rogers.*

★

Index of Contributors

Acknowledgements

"The Willamette" by Kathleen Dean Moore copyright © 1995 by Kathleen
Dean Moore. Reprinted from *Riverwalking: Reflections on Moving Water* with
permission of The Lyons Press.

"Mother to the World" by Cherilyn Parsons published with permission from
the author. Copyright © 1998 by Cherilyn Parsons.

"Where the Desert Blooms" by Janet Strassman Perlmutter published with
permission from the author. Copyright © 1998 by Janet Strassman
Perlmutter.

"The Fourth of July" by Irene-Marie Spencer published with permission from
the author. Copyright © 1998 by Irene-Marie Spencer.

"Vincent's Room" by Christine Loomis originally titled "When We Saw
Vincent van Gogh" reprinted from the September 1986 issue of *Parent's
Magazine*. Copyright © 1986 by Christine Loomis. Reprinted by permis-
sion of the author.

"Mama Bear" by Colin Chisholm reprinted from the March/April 1997 issue
of *Utne Reader*. Copyright © 1997 by Colin Chisholm. Reprinted by permission of the author.

"Nests" by Louise Erdrich excerpted from *The Blue Jay's Dance: A Birth Year* by
Louise Erdrich. Copyright © 1995 by Louise Erdrich. Reprinted by permission of HarperCollins Publishers, Inc. and the author (c/o Charles Rembar,
19 West 44th Street, NY, NY 10036).

"Remembering Dorothy Parker" by Hallie Ephron Touger published with permission from the author. Copyright © 1998 by Hallie Ephron Touger.

"Bambini: Reflections in Venice" by Michele Hanson published with permission from the author. Copyright © 1998 by Michele Hanson.

"Two for the Road" by Molly O'Neill reprinted from the August 10, 1997
issue of *The New York Times*. Copyright © 1997 by The New York Times
Company. Reprinted by permission.

"The Anil Journals" by Susan Wadia-Ells copyright © 1995 by Susan Wadia-
Ells. Reprinted from *The Adoption Reader: Birth Mothers, Adoptive Mothers,
and Adopted Daughters Tell Their Stories* edited by Susan Wadia-Ells and
published by Seal Press.

"Lessons of the Rainforest" by Stephanie Levin-Gervasi published with
permission from the author. Copyright © 1998 by Stephanie Levin-
Gervasi.

Additional Credits (arranged alphabetically by title)

Selections from "Apron Strings" by Pamela Michael reprinted from *Travelers' Tales: Food* edited by Richard Sterling. Reprinted by permission of the author. Copyright © 1997 by Pamela Michael.

Selection from "Bahini and Didi" by Ellie Skeele published with permission from the author. Copyright © 1998 by Ellie Skeele.

Selection from "Bermuda Again" by Jean Ann Pollard published with permission from the author. Copyright © 1998 by Jean Ann Pollard.

Selection from "Big Mothers," by Lynn Ferrin reprinted from the November/December 1981 issue of *Motorland.* Copyright © 1981 by *Motorland.* Reprinted by permission of Motorland/CSAA.

Selection from *The Blue Jay's Dance: A Birth Year* by Louise Erdrich. Copyright © 1995 by Louise Erdrich. Reprinted by permission of HarperCollins Publishers, Inc. and the author (c/o Charles Rembar, 19 West 44th Street, NY, NY 10036).

Selection from "Breathless in Bolivia" by Lynne Cox reprinted from *Travelers' Tales: Women in the Wild* edited by Lucy McCauley. Copyright © 1998 by Lynne Cox.

Selection from "Dancing on the Seine: My Mother's Requiem" by Diane LeBow published with permission from the author. Copyright © 1998 by Diane LeBow.

Poem by Emma Strother published with permission from the author. Copyright © 1998 by Emma Strother.

Selection from *The Fruits of Fifty* by Susan Bistline reprinted by permission of the author. Copyright © 1994 by Susan Bistline. Published by Shreya Press, 1357 Church Street, San Francisco, CA 94114.

Selection from "The Golden Rule and After," *A Preface to Politics* by Walter Lippman published in 1914.

Selection by Sue Willing reprinted from *Gutsy Mamas: Travel Tips and Wisdom for Mothers on the Road* by Marybeth Bond. Reprinted by permission of the author. Copyright © 1997 by Sue Willing.

Selection from "Homemade Rituals of the Goddess" by Rachel Pollack excerpted from an article which originally appeared in the Winter 1997 issue of *Orion* (195 Main St., Great Barrington, MA 01230). Copyright © 1997 by The Myrin Institute.

Selection from "Images" by Suzie Coxhead published with permission from the author. Copyright © 1998 by Suzie Coxhead.

Selection from "Into the Heart of Kashmir" by Virginia Barton Brownback reprinted from the March 19, 1989 issue of *Great Escapes.* Copyright © 1989 by Virginia Barton Brownback.

Selection from *Italian Days* by Barbara Grizzuti Harrison. Copyright © 1989 by Barbara Grizzuti Harrison. Used by permission of Grove/Atlantic, Inc.

Selection from "The Khan Men of Agra" by Pamela Michael reprinted from *Traveler's Tales: A Woman's World* edited by Marybeth Bond. Reprinted by permission of the author. Copyright © 1995 by Pamela Michael.

Selection from *The Very Rich Hours: Travels in Orkney, Belize, the Everglades, and Greece* by Emily Hiestand copyright © 1992 by Emily Hiestand. Reprinted by permission of Beacon Press.

Selections from *Woman and Nature: The Roaring Inside Her* by Susan Griffin copyright © 1978 by Susan Griffin. Reprinted by permission of HarperCollins Publishers, Inc. and the author.

Selection from "Women Who Travel" by Martha Dundon published with permission from the author. Copyright © 1998 by Martha Dundon.

About the Editors

Marybeth Bond and Pamela Michael have almost a century of combined experience—covering a wide range of global travel, mothering, and writing. Marybeth, an "older" mother, had her first child at age 36. Pamela, a "younger" mother, married at 18 and was divorced and raising a child alone at 21. Today she is a grandmother.

Marybeth had explored 40 countries by age 40; at age 40 Pamela hadn't even left the continent. She has made up for lost time since then and has traveled and worked around the world. Both authors work two jobs—Marybeth to feather her nest and Pamela to finance frequent flights from her empty nest.

They both work hard, play hard, and laugh a lot. Somehow, they find ways to indulge their passion for adventurous travel and last fall, while on separate journeys, they managed a one-day rendezvous along the Mekong River in Luang Prabang, Laos.

Marybeth Bond traveled solo around the world for two years at age 30. She has lived in Paris, Luxembourg, and New Caledonia as well as with Sherpa, Ladakhi, and Tibetan families in the Himalayas, an Irish farm family on the Dingle Peninsula, in a Hmong village in northern Vietnam, and among nomads in the Thar Desert in western India. Today she is married to a fellow traveler she met in Kathmandu, has two children, two mortgages, a dog, and dozens of rose bushes. She lives in northern California where she writes, is a consultant, and keynote speaker.

Marybeth's first book, *Travelers' Tales: A Woman's World,* won the Lowell Thomas Gold Medal for Best Travel Book of the year from the Society of American Travel Writers Foundation. Her other books include *Gutsy Mamas* and *Gutsy Women,* which were featured on the *Today Show.* She has appeared extensively on network television (CBS, ABC, NBC) and cable television (CNN, CNBC) as well as National Public Radio.

Pamela Michael is a freelance writer, radio producer, and curriculum development specialist who began travel writing just a few years ago. Her first-ever travel story, "The Khan Men of Agra," won the Book Passage Travel Writing Grand Prize and was published in *Travelers' Tales: A Woman's World.* Since then, her travel pieces have appeared in the *San Francisco Examiner, Odyssey* magazine, *Maiden Voyages,* and other publications. Pamela wrote and produced a four-hour documentary for public radio on Buddhism in the United States, entitled "East Meets West," which is narrated by Richard Gere. She was also the director of the Media/ Education Task Force, an international working group convened by the United Nations. Currently, she is the director of The River of Words Project, an international children's environmental poetry and art contest, which she co-founded with U.S. Poet Laureate (1995-1997) Robert Hass. It is jointly sponsored by International Rivers Network and The Library of Congress Center for the Book. She lives in Berkeley, California.

TRAVELERS' TALES GUIDES

LOOK FOR THESE TITLES IN THE SERIES

Special Interest

THE GIFT OF TRAVEL
THE BEST OF TRAVELERS' TALES
Edited by Larry Habegger, James O'Reilly & Sean O'Reilly
ISBN 1-885211-25-2, 234 pages, $14.95

"The Travelers' Tales series is altogether remarkable."
—Jan Morris

We've selected some favorite stories from the books in our award-winning series, stories about simple but profound gifts travelers have received from people, places, and experiences around the world. *The Gift of Travel* will light a match in the firebox of your wanderlust. Join us on the quest.

THERE'S NO TOILET PAPER ON THE ROAD LESS TRAVELED
THE BEST OF TRAVEL HUMOR AND MISADVENTURE
Edited by Doug Lansky
ISBN 1-885211-27-9, 207 pages, $12.95

"Anyone who plans to travel should read this book. And then stay home."
—Dave Barry

LOVE & ROMANCE
TRUE STORIES OF PASSION ON THE ROAD
Edited by Judith Babcock Wylie
ISBN 1-885211-18-X, 294 pages, $17.95

"...a passion-filled tribute to the undeniable, inescapable romance of the road."

—Debra Birnbaum, Feature Editor, *New Woman*

A DOG'S WORLD
TRUE STORIES OF MAN'S BEST FRIEND ON THE ROAD
Edited by Christine Hunsicker
ISBN 1-885211-23-6, 232 pages, $12.95

"The stories are extraordinary, original, often surprising and sometimes haunting. A very good book."
—Elizabeth Marshall Thomas, author of *The Hidden Life of Dogs*

WOMEN IN THE WILD
TRUE STORIES OF ADVENTURE AND CONNECTION
Edited by Lucy McCauley
ISBN 1-885211-21-X, 307 pages, $17.95

Meet women who foray into the wilderness, explore remote jungle rivers, climb Mt. Everest, and survive a shark attack. Their tales speak the soul's deepest language and show how travel into the wilderness can help you discover the wild woman within.

A MOTHER'S WORLD
JOURNEYS OF THE HEART
Edited by Marybeth Bond and Pamela Michael
ISBN 1-885211-26-0, 234 pages, $14.95

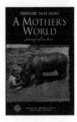

"Heartwarming and heartbreaking, these stories remind us that motherhood is one of the great unifying forces in the world."
—John Flinn, Travel Editor, *San Francisco Examiner*

A WOMAN'S WORLD
Edited by Marybeth Bond
ISBN 1-885211-06-6, 475 pages, $17.95

Winner of the Lowell Thomas Award for Best Travel Book —
Society of American Travel Writers

"I loved this book! From the very first story, I had the feeling that I'd been waiting to read these women's tales for years. I also had the sense that I'd met these women before. I hadn't, of course, but as a woman and a traveler I felt an instant connection with them. What a rare pleasure."
—Kimberly Brown, *Travel & Leisure*

GUTSY WOMEN
TRAVEL TIPS AND WISDOM FOR THE ROAD
By Marybeth Bond
ISBN 1-885211-15-5, 124 pages, $7.95

Packed with instructive and inspiring travel vignettes, *Gutsy Women: Travel Tips and Wisdom for the Road* is a must-have for novice as well as experienced travelers.

GUTSY MAMAS
TRAVEL TIPS AND WISDOM FOR MOTHERS ON THE ROAD
By Marybeth Bond
ISBN 1-885211-20-1, 150 pages, $7.95

A book of tips and wisdom for mothers traveling with their children. This book is for any mother, grandmother, son, or daughter who travels or would like to.

Body & Soul

THE ROAD WITHIN
TRUE STORIES OF TRANSFORMATION

Edited by Sean O'Reilly,
James O'Reilly & Tim O'Reilly
ISBN 1-885211-19-8, 443 pages, $17.95

"Travel is a siren song we are helpless to resist. Heedless of outcomes, we are hooked on the glories of movement, passion and inner growth, souvenirs in abundant supply in *The Road Within*."
—Jeff Salz, *Escape Magazine*

FOOD
A TASTE OF THE ROAD

Edited by Richard Sterling
ISBN 1-885211-09-0, 444 pages, $17.95

"Sterling's themes are nothing less than human universality, passion and necessity, all told in stories straight from the gut."
—Maxine Hong Kingston, author of
The Woman Warrior and *China Men*

THE FEARLESS DINER
TRAVEL TIPS AND WISDOM FOR EATING AROUND THE WORLD

By Richard Sterling
ISBN 1-885211-22-8, 139 pages, $7.95

A pocket companion for those who like to see the world through food. Bold epicures will find all the tips and wisdom needed to feast with savages, break bread with kings, and get invited home to dinner.

Country Guides

BRAZIL

Edited by Annette Haddad & Scott Doggett
ISBN 1-885211-11-2, 433 pages, $17.95
"Only the lowest wattage dimbulb would visit Brazil without reading this book."
—Tim Cahill, author of *Jaguars Ripped My Flesh* and
Pecked to Death by Ducks

NEPAL

Edited by Rajendra S. Khadka
ISBN 1-885211-14-7, 423 pages, $17.95

"Always refreshingly honest, here is a collection that explains why Western travelers fall in love with Nepal and return again and again."
—Barbara Crossette, *New York Times* correspondent and author of
So Close to Heaven: The Vanishing Buddhist Kingdoms of the Himalayas

Country Guides

SPAIN

Edited by Lucy McCauley
ISBN 1-885211-07-4, 452 pages, $17.95

"A superb, eclectic collection that reeks wonderfully of
gazpacho and paella, and resonates with sounds of heel-
clicking and flamenco singing—and makes you feel that you
are actually in that amazing state of mind called Iberia."
—Barnaby Conrad, author of *Matador* and *Name Dropping*

FRANCE

Edited by James O'Reilly,
Larry Habegger & Sean O'Reilly
ISBN 1-885211-02-3, 432 pages, $17.95

"All you always wanted to know about the French but were
afraid to ask! Explore the country and its people in a unique
and personal way even before getting there. Travelers' Tales:
your best passport to France and the French!"
—Anne Sengés, *Journal Français d'Amérique*

INDIA

Edited by James O'Reilly & Larry Habegger
ISBN 1-885211-01-5, 477 pages, $17.95

"The essays are lyrical, magical and evocative:
some of the images make you want to rinse
your mouth out to clear the dust."
—Karen Troianello, *Yakima Herald-Republic*

THAILAND

Edited by James O'Reilly & Larry Habegger
ISBN 1-885211-05-8, 483 pages, $17.95

"This is the best background reading
I've ever seen on Thailand!"
—Carl Parkes, author of *Thailand Handbook*,
Southeast Asia Handbook by Moon Publications

MEXICO

Edited by James O'Reilly & Larry Habegger
ISBN 1-885211-00-7, 426 pages, $17.95

Opens a window on the beauties and mysteries of
Mexico and the Mexicans. It's entertaining,
intriguing, baffling, instructive, insightful, inspiring
and hilarious—just like Mexico."
—Tom Brosnahan, coauthor of
Lonely Planet's *Mexico – a travel survival kit*

City Guides

HONG KONG
Edited by James O'Reilly,
Larry Habegger & Sean O'Reilly
ISBN 1-885211-03-1, 438 pages, $17.95

"*Travelers' Tales Hong Kong* will order and delight the
senses, and heighten the sensibilities, whether you are
an armchair traveler or an old China hand."
—Gladys Montgomery Jones
Profiles Magazine, Continental Airlines

PARIS
Edited by James O'Reilly,
Larry Habegger, & Sean O'Reilly
ISBN 1-885211-10-4, 424 pages, $17.95

"If Paris is the main dish, here is a rich and fascinating
assortment of hors d'oeuvres. *Bon appetit et bon voyage!*"
—Peter Mayle

SAN FRANCISCO
Edited by James O'Reilly,
Larry Habegger & Sean O'Reilly
ISBN 1-885211-08-2, 432 pages, $17.95

"As glimpsed here through the eyes of beatniks, hippies,
surfers, 'lavender cowboys' and talented writers from all
walks, San Francisco comes to vivid, complex life."
—*Publishers Weekly*

SUBMIT YOUR OWN TRAVEL TALE

Do you have a tale of your own that you would like to submit to
Travelers' Tales? We highly recommend that you first read one or more of our
books to get a feel for the kind of story we're looking for. For submission
guidelines and a list of titles in the works, send a SASE to:

Travelers' Tales Submission Guidelines
P.O. Box 610160, Redwood City, CA 94061

or send email to ***ttguidelines@online.oreilly.com***
or visit our web site at **www.oreilly.com/ttales**

You can send your story to the address above or via email to
ttsubmit@oreilly.com. On the outside of the envelope, ***please indicate what
country/topic your story is about***. If your story is selected for one of our titles,
we will contact you about rights and payment.

We hope to hear from you. In the meantime, enjoy the stories!

SUBMIT YOUR OWN TRAVEL TALE

Do you have a tale of your own that you would like to submit to Travelers' Tales? We highly recommend that you first read one or more of our books to get a feel for the kind of story we're looking for. For submission guidelines and a list of titles in the works, send a SASE to:

Travelers' Tales Submission Guidelines
P.O. Box 610160, Redwood City, CA 94061

or send email to *ttguidelines@online.oreilly.com*
or check out our web site at **www.oreilly.com/ttales**

You can send your story to the address above or via email to *ttsubmit@oreilly.com*. On the outside of the envelope, *please indicate what country/topic your story is about*. If your story is selected for one of our titles, we will contact you about rights and payment.

We hope to hear from you. In the meantime, enjoy the stories!

JOURNEY WITH THE WORLD'S BEST TRAVEL WRITERS

Fill in this card and we'll let you know about the best travel stories we've found.

Which book did this card come from? _____

Name _____

Company (optional) _____

Mailing Address _____

City/State _____

Zip/Country _____

Telephone _____

Email address _____

What was your favorite story in this book? _____
_____

We have other Travelers' Tales Guides in the works. What other countries, regions, or topics would you like to see us cover? _____
_____

Why did you buy this book?
☐ Prepare for a trip   ☐ Class/Seminar   ☐ Armchair Travel
☐ Interest in a specific region or topic   ☐ Gift

Where did you purchase your copy?
☐ Bookstore   ☐ Direct from O'Reilly   ☐ Received as gift   ☐ Online   ☐ Other

☐ Please send me the Travelers' Tales Catalog
☐ I do not want my name given to outside mailing lists

Please give us three names and addresses of people you think would like Travelers' Tales.

Name _____
Address _____
City/State/Zip _____

Name _____
Address _____
City/State/Zip _____

Name _____
Address _____
City/State/Zip _____

TRAVELERS' TALES

"Like gourmet chefs sampling the produce in an overstocked French market, the editors of Travelers' Tales pick, sift, and prod their way through the weighty shelves of contemporary travel writing, rejecting the second rate and creaming off the very best. They have impeccable taste — a very welcome addition to the genre."

—*William Dalrymple, author of*
City of Djinns and In Xanadu